A Horse of Course

a Horse of Course

A ROUND UP OF EQUINE FACTS
BY
MARY FRANCES BUDZIK

METRO BOOKS
NEW YORK

This 2008 edition published by Metro Books,
by arrangement with Toucan Books Ltd.

Consultant: William Fortney, DVM
Contributing author: Ben Horslen
Design: Elizabeth Healey
Managing editor: Ellen Dupont
Editor: Marion Dent
Designer: Vivian Foster
Copy editor: Anne McDowall
Editorial assistants: Hannah Bowen, Kathryn Holden, Amy Smith
Indexer: Michael Dent

Metro Books
122 Fifth Avenue
New York, NY 10011

ISBN-13: 978-1-4351-0405-1
ISBN-10: 1-4351-0405-6

Printed and bound in China

1 3 5 7 9 10 8 6 4 2

CONTENTS

CHAPTER 1

The Horse

···

The domesticated horse has played an important part in human

civilization for thousands of years. Thanks to the unremitting labor

of these animals, fields were plowed, wars were fought, and travel by

land—from across the farm to across the continent—became

possible. Yet horses did not evolve with human concerns in mind!

Primitive horses were herd animals happy to graze the days away on

the Asian steppes. As prey animals, their inborn instinct is to flee

predators, such as ourselves—yet over the centuries, such a rapport

between our two species has been established that communication

between horse and rider can be achieved by the subtlest of signals.

THE HORSE'S VITAL SIGNS

VITAL SIGN	IDEAL TEST RESULT	POTENTIAL PROBLEMS
Capillary refill time	Press horse's gums firmly; they'll blanch, but should return to their normal pink color within 1–2 seconds.	Color returns too fast: High blood pressure, agitation, anxiety. Color returns too slowly: Shock, poisoning.
Digital pulse (pulse found in foot)	Take on inside of ankle below fetlock; it should be hard to feel, but detectable.	A strong digital pulse is a symptom of various foot problems, especially laminitis.
Gum color	Pale to bubblegum pink	Pale color indicates anemia; a bluish tinge, a lack of oxygen, which could be a sign of heart disease, lung failure, or colic.
Gut sounds	Long and short rumbles and gurgles	Quiet for longer than two minutes is a bad sign.
Heart rate	30–44 beats per minute	Too fast: Recent exercise, pain, fever, heat stroke, shock, anxiety, heart abnormality. Too slow: Hypothermia, shock, reaction to medication.
Respiratory rate	10–15 breaths per minute	Too fast: Recent exercise, heat stroke, shock, respiratory tract infection, electrolyte imbalance. Too slow: See heart rate.
Temperature	99–101°F (37.2–38.3°C)	Above normal: heat stroke, infection, excess exertion. Below normal: shock, hypothermia.

STARTLING FACTS ABOUT THE HORSE FAMILY

◡ A horse's stomach holds only 2–4 gallons (7.5–15 liters) at a time.

◡ The equine small intestine is about 70 feet (21.3 m) long. (A human's is about 21 feet/6.4 m long.)

◡ A horse's large colon can hold 20–25 gallons (75–95 liters).

◡ Horses cannot vomit or burp, nor are they able to breathe through their mouth.

◡ Most horses have 175 bones in their bodies (see also box below).

◡ Standing at rest, the horse carries between 60 and 70 percent of its weight on its forelimbs.

◡ Horses are the only animals (other than humans) who sweat through their skin.

◡ A horses uses up more energy when it is lying down than it does when standing.

◡ Of all the world's countries, China, Ethiopia, and Mexico have the largest populations of donkeys.

NAME	CLAIM TO FAME	BREED/AREA OF ORIGIN
Chinook	Longest tail: 22 feet (6.7 m)	Palomino/Rhode Island
Maude	Longest mane: 18 feet (5.5 m)	California mare
Old Billy	Oldest: 62 years	English barge horse
Sampson	Tallest and heaviest: 21.5 hands high (7 ft. 2 in./ 21.9 m); 3,360 lb. (1,524 kg)	Shire horse/England

ARABIAN BONES

Most breeds of horse have 18 ribs, 6 lumbar vertebrae, and 18 tail vertebrae, but Arabian horses have only 17 ribs, 5 lumbar vertebrae, and 16 tail vertebrae.

EQUINE FINGERPRINTS

Whorls are spiral-shaped patterns of hair that can grow anywhere on a horse but are most commonly found on its face (often near the forehead) or neck. The Arabian Horse Association, the American Quarter Horse Association, and the Jockey Club (the Thoroughbred registry body) all record individual whorls as a means of identification for registered horses.

◡ No two whorls are alike, so they serve as an "equine fingerprint."

◡ Bedouins, who were great horsemen, used whorls as a way of pricing their horses.

◡ Horse lore states that a horse's character can be divined from the whorl pattern.

◡ Linda Tellington-Jones, a highly respected American trainer and equine behaviorist, has developed a detailed association of personality traits with certain whorl patterns. For example:
• horses with a swirl between the eyes are likely to be uncomplicated
• horses with a swirl beneath the eye are probably intelligent.

I bless the hoss from hoof to head—
From head to hoof, and tale to mane!—
I bless the hoss, as I have said,
From head to hoof, and back again!
JAMES WHITCOMB RILEY (1849–1916), AMERICAN POET

HOW MANY INCHES IN A HAND?

A horse's height is given in "hands"—one hand equals 4 inches (10 cm; the width of an average adult's hand)—and is measured from its shoulders (withers) to its feet. For example, if a horse measures 14.5 hands high (hh), it is 58 inches (147 cm) high.

GALVAYNE'S GROOVES

Sydney "Groove" Galvayne was a horseman of the nineteenth century who once demonstrated his equine skills to Great Britain's Queen Victoria. Galvayne, an Irish-born Australian, made his name with a method of aging horses by evaluating a groove—known today as Galvayne's Groove—that is found on the two corner incisors in the horse's upper jaw.

This groove can be used to age horses from 10 to 30 years old. It first appears at the gum line of a horse at ten years old and moves down the tooth, year by year, as the tooth continues to emerge from the jaw. Up to 4 inches (10 cm) of tooth are embedded in the jawbone, and the tooth slowly grows out of the jaw throughout the horse's life as the teeth are worn down by the grinding action of grazing. So a horse can be aged according to where Galvayne's Groove is on the tooth: at 20, the groove extends the full length of the tooth; by 25, it appears only in the lower half; and, by 30, it has disappeared.

However, Galvayne's method is not foolproof, and there are other aspects of the arrangement and condition of a horse's teeth that are almost as revealing, including the dental cups—shallow depressions on the teeth of young horses that tend to wear away in a predictable pattern. "Bishoping" was a fraudulent method of making older horses appear younger by drilling cups into the teeth, even dyeing them with realistic bacterial stains! Such exhaustive lengths to make a horse appear younger are telling evidence of just how crucial an economic decision buying a horse was in the nineteenth century—every bit as scary and filled with peril as buying a used car is today, in fact.

CHESTNUTS

Sometimes referred to as "night eyes," chestnuts are horny or callouslike growths located just above the knees on the forelegs and just below the hocks on the hinds. Thought to be possibly the vestiges of either toepads or scent glands, the arrangement and shape of these chestnuts—like that of whorls (see page 10)—are unique to each horse.

EQUINE EYESIGHT

Understanding how horses see can help us to interact more safely and effectively with them. In addition, quirks of horse behavior, such as spooking and kicking, can be explained, at least partially, by the way in which horses perceive the world around them.

Ʊ EYES: With large eyes placed high on the sides of the head, horses have almost a 360-degree range of vision. This is at its best when their heads are down as they graze. In addition, the horse's eyes are well adapted to perceive movement.

Ʊ NIGHT VISION: Horses have excellent night vision but need time to adjust to changes from light to dark. This is one reason why you should open trailer side doors and park the trailer in a well-lighted area when you are teaching a horse to load into a trailer.

Ʊ HEAD POSITION: A horse's perception of depth is "flat," which means that with its head down it is unable to gauge distances. This is why it is hard for horses to jump deep fences. However, when a horse raises its head and uses binocular vision to see farther in front, it is able to perceive three dimensions. Head position is obviously important to what a horse sees and this is certainly something to keep in mind as you ride.

Ʊ BLIND SPOTS: A horse's eyes are positioned on the sides of its head, which means that a horse has blind spots. Directly in front of the horse is a triangular-shaped blind spot that extends about 4 feet (1.2 m). This is why it is important always to approach a horse from the side, at the level of its shoulder, so that it can see your face. Similarly, you should never approach a horse from behind. Always speak to your horse when grooming or tacking up, so that it won't be startled if you suddenly emerge from one of its blind spots.

Ʊ MONOCULAR/BINOCULAR VISION: Monocular vision means that horses can see separately with each eye, but, in addition, horses possess binocular vision, which enables them to use both eyes to focus on an object in front of them. Horses cannot use both types of vision at the same time and visual distortion occurs when a horse switches from monocular to binocular vision, or vice versa. This visual distortion can be the cause of "spooking."

CAN A HORSE SWALLOW ITS TONGUE?

Occasionally, when a horse is galloping, it will slow down abruptly and make a gurgling noise in its throat, then it recovers. Old-timers used to claim that the horse had swallowed its tongue. Actually, the problem is caused by the soft membrane in the back of the horse's throat momentarily collapsing and shutting off air flow.

Usually, a horse will recover quickly from such an episode, but if this happens during a race, then all is lost, and the rider may even finish up by flying over the horse's head!

PROUD-CUT GELDINGS

Even after gelding, some horses still act like stallions—herding or even mounting mares, charging "rival" geldings, showing reluctance to separate from mares, and so on. Traditionally, these geldings—castrated male horses—are referred to as "proud cut." It has been claimed that this was because the veterinarian had neglected to remove all of the testicular tissue. More likely, the behavior is due to overactive adrenal glands, which also produce testosterone.

"It is not enough for a man to know how to ride; he must know how to fall."

MEXICAN PROVERB

WHY HORSES GIVE BIRTH AT NIGHT

About 80 percent of mares give birth at night. Thought to be the result of evolution, this survival mechanism meant that a mare would give birth near a herd that was settled for the night, instead of near one traveling in daytime.

Survival is also the reason that mares usually give birth quickly, with a first-stage labor of two to four hours and the actual birth usually completed within an hour. The foal can stand and walk within minutes of birth because, in the wild, both mare and foal must be ready quickly to travel on with the herd.

THE SAD FATE OF EQUINE TWINS

Mares are not well-adapted to carry twins, but some mares (in particular Thoroughbreds and Warmbloods) have a tendency to conceive them. Most twins die in the womb, but if they do survive, they are almost always small and weak— and the mare's health and future breeding potential are often compromised, too.

Ultrasound can detect twins as early as ten days after conception. A vet can then do a rectal examination and manually crush the smaller and weaker of the two embryos, allowing the larger one to survive. Although this seems cruel, it allows the mother and the remaining fetus a much better chance of survival.

Sometimes, however, twins do survive. At the Failte Ireland Dublin horse show, healthy twin mares Thelma and Louise were shown in the foal class— the first time this has happened in the show's 134-year history. The foals were parented by the Irish Draft mare King's Sister and the Thoroughbred Shaandar.

WHEN IT'S TIME TO LEAVE MOTHER

Wild mares do not wean their foals until they are two years old. Domestic foals are usually weaned at five to seven months. Early weaning is highly stressful to both mare and foal—and the foals are much more susceptible to disease during the weaning period.

MAKE MINE A MARE'S MILK!

Kumiss (fermented mare's milk) is a traditional drink of peoples of the Asian steppes. Traditionally, the milk is fermented in a horsehide flask and needs to be churned. Mongolian nomads did this efficiently by securing the flask onto their saddle pads while riding. The Mongols consider kumiss to be an effective aid against a range of diseases. It has a high sugar content, is mildly alcoholic, and has been described as "milk champagne, the great Russian remedy for wasting, debilitating, and nervous diseases."

Russian novelists Tolstoy and Chekov both took "kumiss cures." Tolstoy, particularly fond of the beverage, took the remedy several times, but Chekov's tuberculosis was not cured by the drink. George W. Bush tasted kumiss when visiting Mongolia in 2005, but probably would have preferred chocolate milk!

MAGIC MILT

The milt is said to look like a piece of liver and is present in a foal's mouth at birth. Its purpose is somewhat mysterious, but it may help prevent fluid from entering the mouth and choking the foal during the birth process. Another suggestion is that the milt is related to the formation of the horse's tongue.

Rural legend says the milt should be dried and placed on the stable roof as a magical protection to all within. Native American medicine men and rural horse whisperers (see page 95) also considered dried milt to have healing power.

THE CREAM GENE

The cream gene is a color modification (or dilution) gene that is found in two places within the horse's genetic code. A single cream gene makes a horse's base color one shade lighter; two cream genes make it two shades lighter.

⋃ BASIC COLORS: Chestnut, bay, sorrel, and black are basic colors; horses of these colors have no cream gene present in their genetic code.

⋃ SINGLE DILUTES: Palominos (chestnut with one cream gene), buckskins (bay with one cream gene), and smoky black (black with one cream gene) horses are known as "single dilutes," showing the effect of a single cream gene.

⋃ DOUBLE DILUTES: Cremellos and Perlinos are known as "double dilutes," which means that they have two cream genes in their genetic code. The effect of these genes is to give these horses pink skin, blue eyes, and light cream color coats. Cremellos are chestnuts with two cream genes and have white manes and tails. Perlinos, which are bays with two cream genes, have an orangish mane, tail, and lower legs.

THE DUN FACTOR

The "dun factor" is another color modification gene. Dun horses usually have a yellowish or tan coat with darker-colored mane, tail, and markings.

GRULLA (from the Spanish word for "gray crane"): A black horse "diluted" by one dun gene, this horse is mouse colored—each hair is of that mousey color (the coat is not a mixture of white and black hairs).

PRIMITIVE MARKINGS: Grullas also usually have "primitive markings"; in other words, they have a dorsal stripe (extending down the middle of the back, sometimes through the mane and tail), shoulder and/or leg striping (like zebra stripes), facial "cobwebbing," and ears with darker tips.

SHADES OF GRAY

Gray horses have dark skin and white, or mixed white and dark, hair. A gray horse can be any number of gray shades—light or dark, dappled, speckled, even tinted with rose—but its coat often lightens during its lifetime.

◡ LIGHT GRAY: The skin around the eyes, nose, inside the ears, and between the hind legs is black. Light gray horses are often mistaken for white ones but can be distinguished by their dark skin.

◡ STEEL GRAY: Dark silver gray, with a black base coat made up of a mixture of white and gray hairs. Steel grays sometimes lighten and turn dapple or light gray as they age.

◡ DAPPLE GRAY: The marks on a dapple gray look as though they have been made with a small sponge. Dapple grays are usually dappled all over, with darker points, on a steel gray base.

◡ FLEA-BITTEN GRAY: A light gray body, with evenly distribued speckles of black or brown.

◡ ROSE GRAY: A medium gray that is tinted with red or rose. The points, including the mane and tail, are often darker.

NOT TO BE CONFUSED WITH ... ROAN

Roan horses can sometimes be mistaken for grays. A roan has white hairs on a dark background; grays continue to lighten as they age, but roans do not.

HORSE TALK

Horses like to communicate vocally with one another, by using a variety of sounds—from snorts and squeals to neighs and nickers. The following are a few of the ways in which they talk to each other.

SNORT: A powerful exhalation that sounds both curious and concerned is used to signal that danger may be near. A snorting horse will probably face in the direction of the threat, so the herd is warned by both sound and body language.

BLOW: A milder exhalation of air, often used when a horse is being ridden and, therefore, is exerting himself, but not to excess.

SQUEAL: This defensive signal is often used when two horses who are strangers meet. It's an aggressive warning that may be bluster or serious. Mares also squeal when introduced to a stallion for mating, but it's usually a preliminary "I'm not easy, you know" signal!

NICKER (GREETING): This low, chuckling sound is used between two horse friends. It is also used to greet a human friend, especially at feeding time, as a reminder: "I'm here and I'm hungry!" Nickers are positive anticipatory sounds. ("Whicker" is another word for nicker.)

NICKER (COURTSHIP): Stallions do this when approaching a mare. It's the stallion version of "Hey, baby!"

NICKER (MATERNAL): A mare will nicker to her foal when she is concerned about its safety, as a kind of call to "come back to mama."

NEIGH: Longer, louder, and screechier than the nicker, the neigh expresses concern and is used when a horse has been separated from, or wants to locate, the herd. A horse may neigh, for example, if it has been left in the barn when its buddy is turned out, or it has been put out to pasture and wants to know where everyone is. The herd may reply with an "Over here, we're up on the farthest slope!" neigh of its own.

WHINNY: This is a gentler, sadder neigh, which carries with it an overtone of longing.

ROAR: Rare in domestic horses, the roar may be given by wild horses that are fighting intensely, very fearful, or in emotional shock.

THE HORSE LAUGH

When a horse is investigating an interesting smell, it may lift, wrinkle, and flutter its upper lip in what looks like a sneer, a grimace, or a "horse laugh." You may notice such behavior in a stallion toward a mare that is in heat, for example, or in a mare with her newborn foal.

This reflex, which is known as flehmening (from a German root word meaning "to curl"), can be misunderstood as aggressive, because the horse's incisors are typically bared as the lips are drawn back—hence the "laugh." In fact, the flehmen motion draws scent pheromones back toward chemical receptors that are located on the roof of the mouth. Chemical "messages" trigger electrical impulses that send information to the horse's brain—such as "This mare is in season!" or "This little foal is mine!"

The flehmen response is well developed in other hoofed mammals (ungulates), too, as well as in felines. You may notice a cat behaving in a similar way.

A horse is a thing of beauty . . . none will tire of looking at him as long as he displays himself in his splendor.
XENOPHON (C.435–C.354 B.C.)
SPARTAN OFFICER

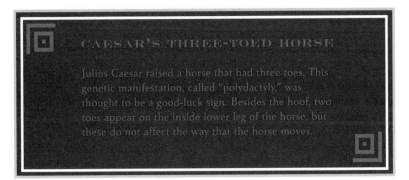

CAESAR'S THREE-TOED HORSE

Julius Caesar raised a horse that had three toes. This genetic manifestation, called "polydactyly," was thought to be a good-luck sign. Besides the hoof, two toes appear on the inside lower leg of the horse, but these do not affect the way that the horse moves.

GETTING YOUR HORSE'S TEMPERATURE

To the horse novice, it would seem that horses are often categorized by the temperature of their blood—yet all horses actually have the same body temperature, between 99°F and 101°F (37.2°C and 38.3°C). Referring to a horse's blood temperature is, in fact, a way of describing its temperament.

HOTBLOODS	WARMBLOODS	COLDBLOODS
Main breeds are Arabians and Thoroughbreds (the latter are sometimes referred to as "blood" horses)	Main breeds include Hanoverian, Trakehner, Selle Français, Oldenburg, and Danish, Dutch, and American Warmbloods	Main breeds are Belgian Heavy Draft, Clydesdale, Shire, and Suffolk Punch
Quick, sensitive, easily spooked, a strongly developed flight instinct	The result of crossing hot-blooded Arabian, Spanish, and Mongolian breeds with heavier Northern European horses	Large, powerful horses bred for farm work
Superb performance horses in the right hands	Popular in horse-show disciplines, particularly dressage	Noted for their easygoing temperaments

The association of temperament with a particular breed is by no means a sure thing. It is perfectly possible to find a "hot-tempered" Warmblood, for example, or even a Thoroughbred so calm that you'd swear he was a plow horse in another life!

THE HORSE'S TRAGIC ADDICTION

One of the most dangerous weeds that a horse can eat is the locoweed, a pealike plant of the Astralagus and Oxytropis generas that is common throughout the West, from Canada down to Mexico. About 20 of the many locoweed species are poisonous—one species identified in Nevada is so toxic that it poisons even the bees pollinating the plant. Indeed, locoism is so notorious that the expression to "go loco" is sometimes used to describe any animal or human who is behaving oddly.

Horses who eat locoweed often become obsessed, searching it out and refusing to touch anything else. A locoweed-addicted horse will wander aimlessly, often in circles, exhibit altered gaits (including bizarrely high steps), and generally show erratic behavior. It may misjudge objects, taking a great leap just to walk over a small log, or attempt to rear and end up sitting on its hind ends like a dog. A horse who has locoweed poisoning may appear lethargic one minute, then may suddenly become frantic about nothing more than a leaf blowing in the wind, or a bird landing in a field.

Horses may recover to some extent from locoweed poisoning if they are removed from all access to the plant at an early enough stage, but they will probably never behave completely normally, and they are dangerous to ride.

> *There is a touch of divinity even in brutes,*
> *and a special halo about a horse, that should*
> *forever exempt him from indignities.*
> HERMAN MELVILLE (1819–91), AMERICAN NOVELIST

CLONED HORSES

Cloning involves taking the genetic material from cells of a donor animal and then implanting it in a donor egg whose own genetic material has been removed. The cloned embryos are grown for a short while in an incubator before being transferred to a surrogate mare.

CLONED HORSES: The first cloned horse was Prometea, a Haflinger foal, born May 28, 2003, in Cremona, Italy. Prometea's birth mother was the donor of her genetic material, although this is not usually the case with cloned horses. Since Prometea's birth, other performance horses have also been cloned:

• *ET,* winner of two world show-jumping championships
• *Pieraz,* a gelding and world champion endurance horse
• *Royal Blue Boon,* a champion Quarter Horse mare who has won more than $380,000 and whose traditionally borne children have won more than $2 million (Royal Blue Boon was beyond safe natural breeding age when she was cloned)
• *Scamper,* a gelding and winner of ten world championship barrel-racing titles.
• *Tap O Lena,* a cutting horse, winner of more than $450,000.

Owners say that their clones will be used for breeding to pass on the superior genetic material instead of for competition. Cloning costs up to $150,000, but for owners it is good economics—breeding and sales fees for superior animals are high.

THE CASE AGAINST CLONING: Most purebred registries are wary of cloning. The Jockey Club (the Thoroughbred registry) will not accept horses born from artificial insemination, let alone clones. The only Throughbreds allowed to race or to be registered come from completely natural breedings. The American Cutting Horse Association allows clones or their descendants to compete, but the American Quarter Horse Association does not currently register clones.

Registries and others are understandably apprehensive because the long-term effects of cloning are still uncertain. They also claim that breeding what is essentially the same horse over and over will not improve the breed, and they argue that the "art" of breeding will disappear if breeders simply clone the best animals.

WHY MULES ARE RARELY MOTHERS

Mules are generally reckoned to be sterile, although several female mules have produced offspring when mated to a purebred horse or ass. Since 1527, there have been more than 60 foals born to female mules around the world and probably others that have not been documented. Most recently, Kate, a pack mule in Colorado, gave birth in July 2007.

The reason that mules rarely produce young successfully is that their parents—they have donkey fathers and horse mothers—have different numbers of chromosomes, and these have different structures. While horses have 64 chromosomes, donkeys have only 62. Mules have 63 chromosomes that are a mixture of ones from each parent. The different structure and number of chromosomes usually prevent them from pairing up and creating successful embryos.

HOW ONE HORSE'S BLOOD IS HELPING TO CURE DISEASE

Twilight, a Thoroughbred mare stabled at Cornell University in Ithaca, New York, has contributed her DNA via blood sample to an important project that has enabled scientists to map one million genetic variation "signposts" for both ancestral and modern horse breeds. Variation maps help veterinary researchers understand the genetic causes of breed-related diseases as well as their behavior differences. In addition, the findings from Twilight's DNA should aid human biomedical researchers—there are at least 80 equine genetic problems that relate to similar disorders in human beings.

GREAT-HEARTED HORSES

Winning racehorses traditionally have been said to have "great heart," and the phrase is literally true. The average horse heart weighs 8½ pounds (3.9 kg), but autopsies of racehorses have shown that they usually have larger hearts.

The largest heart of all weighed a whopping 22 pounds (10 kg); it belonged to the supreme Triple Crown champion Secretariat. After he died, his heart was found to be perfectly healthy and was described by the doctor who performed the autopsy as being a "great engine."

The fabled Eclipse, who died in 1764, was the first racehorse noted to have a large heart—his weighed 14 pounds (6.4 kg). An influential sire, Eclipse is thought to have passed the large heart characteristic down through the female line.

The large heart trait is carried by a gene found on the x chromosome, and can be passed either by a stallion to his daughters or by a dam to her colts. Females who carry a double factor for the x chromosome are highly prized as brood mares because they are more likely to pass on the trait. Inheritance of the large heart gene is one reason for Secretariat's daughters being more successful racehorses than his sons.

Famous Quarter Horse sires who carry the large heart characteristic and were descended from Eclipse include Leo, Three Bars, Go Man Go, and Depth Charge. The fabled Phar Lap, foaled in New Zealand and raced in Australia, also had a heart weighing 14 pounds (6.4 kg).

The size of the heart does not correlate with the size of the horse.

Heart size in a living horse can be determined by ultrasound. Today, the literal heart size of racehorses is scored on a scale, and a high score can increase the horse's worth.

Horses also have outsize spleens, which release extra richly oxygenated red blood cells into the bloodstream, virtually on demand, when horses run. By contrast, human athletes have to train at high altitudes in order to produce extra red blood cells. The equine heart is adapted to pump the thicker, more viscous blood that results from an increase of up to 50 percent in red blood cells.

THE ANATOMY OF THE HORSE

L ike people, horses have shoulders, forearms, and backs. However, these body parts don't function in the same way as ours—we don't generally walk on our forearms, for example, and unlike a human back, a horse's doesn't bend (which is why it's hard for a horse to get up after resting). Equine eyesight is very different from ours, too (see page 12). Unlike us, horses have cannons and pasterns, hocks, and withers. Take a look at the drawing below and you'll never be baffled by the lingo of horse anatomy. You'll learn the difference between a fetlock and a footlock, and find out where the chestnut (see page 11) is.

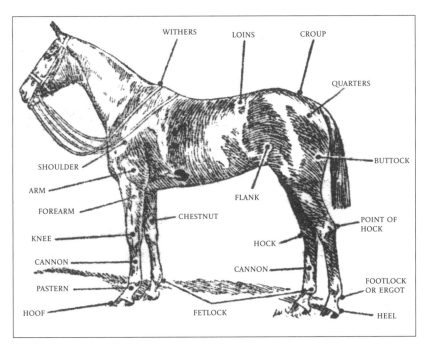

WHY HORSES CAN SLEEP STANDING UP

You may have noticed that once horses lie down, it is not easy for them to get up again. They cannot leap lightly to their feet. Instead, they raise their forehand first and then heave the rest of themselves up. Horses actually expend ten percent less energy standing up than they do lying down, precisely opposite to ruminant grazers, such as cattle or sheep.

The so-called "stay" apparatus, unique to horses, means that they can rest standing up without having to expend energy. Like a folding card table, horses can "lock" their limbs. In the forelimbs, the tendons have a groove that locks into the humerus; in the hind limbs, the patella locks into a crest on the femur.

Horses do need to lie down, but not often, maybe two hours over the course of a couple of days. This enables them to achieve REM (rapid eye movement) sleep. If deprived of REM sleep over a very long period, they would eventually doze off involuntarily and their knees would buckle.

"EAT-AND-RUN" GRAZING

Horses obtain only 70 percent as much energy from a given amount of forage as do grazing ruminants, such as cows and sheep.

◯ Unlike ruminants, horses do not need to rest after grazing. This is because they have an organ in the gut called the cecum, which breaks down indigestible cellulose in grass. Cows need to rechew what they graze ("chewing the cud"). Horses share this "eat-and-run" capability with tapirs and rhinoceroses.

◯ Horses make up for the lower amount of energy they extract from their food by being able to take in a larger quantity of forage throughout the day. Because they can increase quantity to make up for poor quality, they can survive on lower quality grazing than cows or sheep.

CAN HORSES SWIM?

Horses can swim, but it's hard work! Swimming horses move their limbs in an action that looks like a pacing gait, with the legs moving in lateral pairs. A well-conditioned horse can swim for up to 20 minutes, but will use much more energy to move through water than it would moving the same distance on land. A 500-yard (457-m) swim is equal to a mile's gallop.

◡ The pressure of the water on the ribcage and the lungs is what makes the cardiovascular workout of swimming so intense for horses.

◡ Because there is no shock impact or stress to the limbs, swimming is good therapy for horses with muscle or joint injuries.

◡ For the same reason, pools are used to keep horses from injuring themselves after operations or when they are waking up from anesthesia. When famous racehorse Barbaro woke up after having an operation on his leg, following the accident that ended his career in 2006, he found himself in a specially designed water tank, which kept him from reinjuring himself.

◡ For therapeutic purposes, horses swim in cool water. This helps to dissipate the large amount of heat that horses generate while swimming.

PULLING ALL-NIGHTERS

Equine sleep patterns have evolved to keep horses safe. Originally native to plains and steppes, horses could be preyed upon—not conducive to a good night's rest! In fact, most horses sleep just 2 to 3 hours in a 24-hour period, and much of that time is taken in brief naps. Wild horses within a herd actually sleep better than stabled horses, because they have the security of herd "sentinels" to depend on. The more isolated a horse is from close contact with other horses, the more he will feel that he has to be on the alert at all times.

THE FIRST HORSES

It was probably in North America that horses evolved from a small fawnlike, forest-dwelling, multitoed, leaf-eating animal, *Pliohippus,* to their present form, *Equus caballus.* For unknown reasons—perhaps due to climate change—they all migrated over the ancient land bridge from Alaska to Siberia.

By the first millennium B.C., the steppes of Eurasia had become home to the earliest horses. These primitive ponylike equines were compact and robust with thick muscular necks and short broad heads. The Przewalski and the Tarpan were their descendents.

THE PRZEWALSKI (sha-val-ski), or Asiatic Wild Horse, is named after N. M. Przewalski, a Russian explorer who discovered a herd at the edge of the Gobi desert in 1881. Also known as the Takhi, the Przewalski is a stocky yellow dun with dark points. Some have called the Przewalski the ancestor of modern horse breeds, but it is a different species from the domestic horse. Like the zebra, it is difficult to tame or train.

THE TARPAN was the wild horse of Europe, ranging as far east as the Ukrainian steppes. After the Przewalski horse was shown to have a different genetic makeup, the Tarpan was cited as the most likely ancestor of the modern European horse. It is light gray in color with a black dorsal stripe. Tarpans existed in the wild in Poland in the nineteenth century, but were killed off because they were disruptive to domestic herds of horses. The Polish government has since collected and bred these "Tarpan types" in an attempt to recreate the Tarpan.

THE HUCUL, a type of pony from the Carpathian region of Poland, has direct Tarpan ancestry. Wild herds of Hucul (known locally as the Carpathian Pony) still wander the mountains. Selective breeding, and the introduction of Arab blood, is practiced at stud farms—notably near Gorlice in southern Poland.

THE CELTIC (or Atlantic) Pony, first described 1904, is similar to today's Exmoor.

THE NORSE HORSE is thought to be the Vikings' horse, and also the ancestor of the Norwegian Fjord. This popular breed bears a striking resemblance to early types and has the dorsal stripe of the Tarpan.

RUNNING WILD

Almost all wild horse herds throughout the world are composed of feral horses—that is, horses descended from domesticated stock that then escaped or were released into the wild. The only horses never known to be domesticated are the Przewalski and the original Tarpan. The table below lists some of the world's best-known "wild" horses.

BREED	WHERE THEY ROAM
BRUMBY	Australia: Notably in the Australian Alps in the southeast, in Northern Territory, and in Queensland.
CARMARGUE	France: In the Rhone River delta, where they are the mounts of Carmargue "cowboys."
DÜLMEN	Germany: On the Duke of Croy's reserve in Westphalia.
FELL PONY	Great Britain: Mountains and moorlands, particularly in Cumbria. Although Fell Ponies are traditionally owned— the Royal family has a herd in Scotland, for example— they are allowed to run free.
MUSTANG	United States: Highest populations are in Nevada; also in Colorado, Montana, Oregon, and Utah. Most herds are managed by the Bureau of Land Management.
NEW FOREST PONY	Great Britain: In the New Forest, Hampshire, where they are owned by the commoners of the Forest.
PRZEWALSKI	Mongolia, but not seen in the wild since 1968. Now introduced to North Wales (Great Britain), the Ukraine, South Australia, and the Wilds Wildlife Preserve in Cumberland, Ohio. (Today's Przewalski's horses— numbering about 1,200— have all been bred from 13 captive horses after they nearly became extinct.)

DOMESTICATED BREEDS

Many countries have their own breeds of horses—from Argentina's Falabella to England's Suffolk Punch. Each breed has been adapted for particular uses and is defined by its size, body shape, and coat color. There are numerous breeds worldwide; a few of the best-known are detailed below.

BREED	KEY CHARACTERISTICS	HISTORY
AKHAL TEKE	Slim, long-bodied, thin-skinned, and with a long, narrow head and sparse mane and tail. Its coat, usually pale gold, has a metallic bloom. A superior long-distance horse, with tremendous endurance, it is used in show jumping, horse racing, and dressage.	The breed was developed by tribesmen in Turkmenistan. In 1935, 15 Akhal Tekes made an 84-day, 2,600-mile (4,185-km) trip from Ashkabad to Moscow. The Akhal Teke stallion Absent won medals in three Olympic games during the 1960s.
BASHKIR CURLY (also known as American Curly Horse, or Curly Horse)	Some have tightly curled coats, curly eyelashes, and dreadlocked manes. Others have normal body coats, but curls inside their ears and at the fetlocks, together with a kinky mane and tail.	Native American art shows curly-haired horses at the Battle of the Little Bighorn (1876). The Damele family, horse breeders from Nevada, are believed to have given the breed the name "Bashkir."
FALABELLA	Short, about 30 inches (76 cm at the withers), but proportioned like a tiny Arabian horse. It has a luxurious mane and tail, and a long, silky coat. Spotted, gray Appaloosa patterns are most popular.	In 1963, Robert Kennedy imported several of these horses from Argentina and gave them to his children for Christmas. They were later photographed on the White House lawn.

BREED	KEY CHARACTERISTICS	HISTORY
KIGER MUSTANG	These horses, which are mostly duns with primitive markings, have a striking appearance and a high-stepping gait. A luxurious tail confirms the breed's Spanish origins, as does a prominent eel stripe along its back.	A breed promoted as an unexpected result of the 1971 Wild Free Roaming Horse and Burro Act. Roundups of wild herds in Oregon led to genetic testing at the University of Kentucky, which confirmed their relationship to the Iberian strains of horses first brought to the Americas by Spanish explorers.
MARSH TACKY	Canny, sure-footed horses, with refined heads and long manes and tails.	The official horse breed of South Carolina was used in the 1800s for hunting wild game. Feral herds existed on barrier islands and salt marshes in Colonial times. Genetic testing has confirmed their Iberian ancestry.
PERCHERON	Predominantly dapple-gray colored horses, with long, arched necks, thick manes, and powerful hind quarters. The Percheron is one of only two "clean-legged" (no feathering) Draft horse breeds.	From northern France, Percherons were crossbred with Arabs from the 1100s. Used as an artillery horse in World War I battlefields, as a coach horse, and as a farm horse, the breed is popular worldwide, particularly in the United States and Canada.
SUFFOLK PUNCH	Chestnut coloring varies in shade from light to dark. Like the Percheron, this large and strong breed is "clean-legged."	Developed as a farm horse, typically pulling plows in the heavy clay soils of Suffolk, eastern England, during the late 1700s.

THE BAROQUE HORSE BREEDS

Because of their beauty and presence, these horses are named after the extravagant and ornamental "Baroque" style of art and architecture. They are renowned for their elegant profiles, strong, arched necks, and long, thick manes and tails.

ANDALUSIAN: Developed in Spain, these horses are used as bullfighting horses and as herders.

AZTECA: The national horse of Mexico was developed in the 1970s as a cross of the Andalusian and the American Quarter Horse (the first all-American breed). The Azteca is used in dressage and in "cow-work."

FRIESIAN: This breed from the Netherlands is used as a farm horse and as a carriage horse.

LIPIZZAN: Developed in the former Austro-Hungarian Empire, the Lipizzan is the star of the Spanish Riding School in Vienna, Austria, and also serves as a carriage horse. Almost all Lipizzans are gray.

LUSITANO: Originally developed to be ridden in battle, this Portuguese version of the Andalusian is now used in the bullring, as a carriage horse, and for dressage. The Conquistadors are said to have brought the Lusitano with them to the Americas.

ENDANGERED BREEDS

Critically threatened horse breeds include the Caspian Horse, the American Cream Draft, the Cleveland Bay Horse, the Exmoor Pony, the Florida Cracker Horse, and the Suffolk Punch.

ZEEDONK, ZORSE, AND OTHER FAMILY MEMBERS

Zebras, horses, and donkeys are all part of the Equidae family and can interbreed, leading to a fascinating family tree of names.

 JACKASS: A male donkey.

 JENNY: A female donkey (also known as a jennet).

 MULE: Offspring of a male donkey and a female horse.

 HINNY: Offspring of a male horse and a female donkey.

 JOHNS: Male mules.

 MOLLIES: Female mules.

 ZEBROID: Generic term for any equine hybrid with zebra ancestry.

 ZEEDONK: A zebra/donkey hybrid. Also known as a zebrass, zebronkey, zonkey, zebadonk, zenkey, zebrule, or deebra.

 ZETLAND: A zebra/Shetland pony hybrid.

 ZORSE: A zebra/horse hybrid, offspring of a zebra stallion and a horse mare.

THE QUAGGA

South African equine related to the horse and zebra, the quagga *(Equus quagga)* disappeared about 150 years ago, after being hunted to extinction. The front half of the quagga was striped like a zebra, while its back half was a solid dun color like that of a horse.

Thanks to DNA taken from a quagga pelt and a skeleton in the Yale Peabody Museum, it now seems almost certain that quaggas evolved from a species of plains zebra. These animals had become isolated from other zebras during the Ice Age and went on to develop their own particular coat pattern, possibly due to a number of factors resulting from their physical isolation.

CHAPTER 2

Famous Horses

....

Horses are beautiful, powerful animals, and they seem to possess a charisma that draws people to them even when we no longer have a practical need for their working abilities. Many compelling human personalities, from great generals, such as Alexander the Great and Ulysses S. Grant, to enigmatic beauty Jacqueline Kennedy Onassis, and royal icon Queen Elizabeth II, have been irresistibly drawn to the horse. Some canny horses have also managed to make a name for themselves in show business, such as wise talkers Mr. Ed and Francis the Mule and the erudite "Beautiful Jim Key"!

BLACK BEAUTY

Anna Sewell (1820–78) lived only a few months after the publication of her enchanting novel *Black Beauty* (1877), which was an immediate bestseller. Today, it is still a much-loved children's classic. Anna, born in England into a Quaker family, was an invalid, unable to walk following a childhood fall. She helped her mother, a popular children's novelist, with her books—and every day she drove her father to work in a horse and carriage. It was said Anna could control the horses with her voice alone.

HER LOVE OF HORSES

Anna wrote *Black Beauty* for people who work with horses to influence them to be kind. The book is written in the voice of Beauty, a cheerful horse given a good upbringing, who always tries his best. He is a sharp observer of the behavior of the humans who control his fate. His comments on the brutal way in which horses were treated led to the outlawing in England of the check (or bearing) rein, a tight rein that held the heads of carriage horses at a painful upright angle to make them look spirited. Many of Beauty's points about the cruelties to which horses were subjected are made via his descriptions of what he sees other horses suffer:

• Beauty's dear friend, the spirited chestnut mare Ginger, is driven to death by overwork and harsh treatment.

• Sir Oliver, a dignified cob, has had his tail docked short—for fashion—so that he is at the mercy of biting flies.

• Beauty's brother, Rob Roy, has his neck broken during a hell-bent foxhunt.

SAGE ADVICE

The book points out that ignorance, as well as outright cruelty, can cause pain to innocent horses. Beauty himself becomes desperately ill when Little Joe Green, a well-meaning but ignorant stable boy, does not properly cool him after a hard night's ride, when Beauty and good John Manley bring a doctor to Squire Gordon's ill wife. Years later, a wiser Joe Green redeems himself when he nurses a much older Beauty, now in a terrible physical condition, back to health.

A Horse misused upon the Road Calls to Heaven for Human blood.
WILLIAM BLAKE (1757–1827), ENGLISH POET

MR. ED

Mr. Ed, a television show about a Palomino horse who talked only to his owner, was a classic 1960s' sitcom that ran from 1961 to 1966. It starred Alan Young as Wilbur, an architect who worked from home, Connie Hines as Carol, his wife, and a former show and parade Palomino horse, named Bamboo Harvester, as Ed. Mr. Ed rode roughshod over Wilbur in the series—helping Wilbur with his taxes, offering advice about dealing with the neighbors, and making Carol more than a little jealous.

A popular rumor that Mr. Ed was really a zebra (supposedly not evident on black-and-white television) is untrue. Ed "talked" by means of a thread placed under his upper lip; when the thread (not visible on screen) was pulled, Ed fluttered his lips. A star of many talents, Mr. Ed had two recording hits in the 1960s—"Pretty Little Filly" and "Empty Feedbag Blues"—but his voice was actually that of Alan "Rocky" Lane, star of the television show *Red Rider* (1956) and Western movies. Clint Eastwood was an early guest star on *Mr. Ed*. Ed's understudy, Pumpkin, later appeared on *Green Acres* with Eva Gabor.

QUICK DRAW MCGRAW

Quick Draw McGraw was one of the Hanna-Barbera* cartoon characters, another staple of Saturday morning kids' television shows in the 1960s.

The Quick Draw character (a parody of a western sheriff) was a white horse who walked on two legs and was decked out in a holster and ten-gallon hat. His sidekick and deputy, Baba Looey, was a burro with a Mexican accent.

The oddity of the Quick Draw cartoons was that although Quick Draw was undoubtedly a horse, he often rode a horse—an ordinary horse who walked on four legs and was not a caricature—in cartoon episodes, or he sometimes drove a stagecoach pulled by horses. This "horses riding horses" motif is unusual.

---

*William Denby Hanna (1910–2001) and Joseph Roland Barbera (1911–2006) were masters of television cartoon animation series, including *Huckleberry Hound, The Flintstones,* and *Tom and Jerry.*

FRANCIS
THE TALKING MULE

Francis the Talking Mule starred in seven 1950s' comedy motion pictures based on a novel by David Stern and directed by Arthur Lubin, who had worked on Abbot and Costello movies and the *Mr. Ed* television series. "Francis" was a female mule named Molly (bought for just $350), who showed a multimillion dollar profit for Universal Studios. Like Mr. Ed, Francis moved his lips thanks to the invisible thread (under the lips) that was tugged during the mule's dialogue sequences. A folksy, rumble-voiced Texan called Chill (this is Texas humor—he was born on the hottest day of 1903) Wills provided the voice. Francis also made cameo appearances in the *Ma and Pa Kettle* movies.

SAGE ADVICE

An experienced army mule, Francis has seen it all. His sage, cynical advice helps raw Army recruit Peter Stirling (played by Donald O'Connor, 1925–2003)—get ahead in the army (by passing on strategy overheard from Generals) or win at the track (he shoots the breeze with horse buddies at the track). When Peter  says that his inside tips came from a mule, he is sent to an army psychiatrist, and ends up weaving baskets (a remedy for calming mental patients at that time).

REMEMBERING FRANCIS

These movies poking mild fun at the army were sweet relief to Americans recovering from the hardships of World War II. Francis souvenirs included horseshoes emblazoned "Francis: the greatest comedy to come out of the war," buttons claiming "I talked to Francis the talking mule," a Francis puppet (in a plaid army issue horse blanket), and Francis comics. O'Connor quit after the fifth Francis movie, complaining that the mule got more fan mail than he did! The final Francis flick was *Francis in the Haunted House* (1956).

HI-YO SILVER!

Silver, the famous horse ridden by the masked Lone Ranger in the successful 1950s' television series, was introduced by a melodramatic voice as: "A fiery horse with the speed of light, a cloud of dust, and a hearty hi-yo Silver, Away!"—cue the gallop music, with thundering hoofs.

There were actually two Silvers: Silver no. 1 was a Morab (Arab/Morgan cross) of a dazzling gray color. Luckily, for an impressive 17-hands-high horse who had to rear, paw the sky, and gallop at full speed along mountain passes as part of his day job, this Silver was gentle. However, Silver no. 2, an Arab/Saddlebred (today called a National Show Horse) was temperamental. He hated the sound of rolling cameras, and he was a stallion. In fact, his stunt double, Traveler, was the horse used whenever the Lone Ranger had to leap from the horse at full gallop (a frequent occurrence). Silver no. 1 retired in 1956; Silver no. 2 died in 1974 at age 29.

TRIGGER & BUTTERMILK

Trigger (1932–65), a 15.3-hand Palomino stallion from the Hudkins Ranch (co-owned by Bing Crosby), which supplied horses for movies, was mostly Thoroughbred. He was in 80 movies and 100 Roy Rogers television episodes. Rogers (1911–98) renamed him—he was originally called Golden Cloud—after sidekick Smiley Burnette commented that the horse was "quick off the trigger."

Not as quick, however, as Buttermilk (1941–72), Dale Evans' Quarter Horse, a light buckskin gelding with dark points. Buttermilk was said to be faster in a quick dash to the rescue than Trigger—Quarter Horses got their name because they were experts at quarter-mile races—and television scenes had to be reshot because Buttermilk was not supposed to be in the lead—this was the 1950s, after all! Amazingly, Dale Evans (1912–2001) was unable to ride before she met Roy. Trigger's first appearance with Roy was in *Under Western Skies* (1945), and his movie swan song was in *Son of Paleface* with Bob Hope (1957).

BALAAM'S ASS

The only animal in the entire Bible (besides the snake) given the power of speech is Balaam's Ass—and the ass comes off much the superior moral being in his exchanges with the prophet Balaam!

It is the ass who sees the angel with upraised sword blocking the road, while Balaam remains blind to it. Three times the ass moves aside from the angel; each time he is beaten mercilessly by Balaam. Finally, the ass (lying down and refusing to move) speaks: "What have I done to thee, that thou hast struck me three times . . . have I ever failed thee?" Balaam has to admit that the ass has never failed him. Again, the ass upbraids Balaam: "Am not I thine ass upon which thou hast ridden all thy life long?" Balaam, now humbled, is forced to admit that it is his mere ass who speaks the truth after the Lord opens his eyes and he, too, sees the angel. Thus, equines speak for truth and for faithfulness in the Bible itself.

JUSTA BOB

Justa Bob, a racehorse in *Horse Heaven*, Jane Smiley's novel of all things racehorse and track-related, is spiritual kin to Balaam's Ass—a truth teller.

Justa Bob usually wins his races by a nose ("justa bob")—and because Smiley writes about Justa Bob in his own voice, readers feel he is speaking directly to them. His view of life at the track as a claimer (ordinary racehorse) is nothing fancy; he just sees things squarely and is never mean. About the most nefarious action Justa Bob takes is to "manure" in his water bucket (sound familiar, all you horse owners?), when he has to make a sardonic comment on the at-the-mercy-of-the-humans life of a reliable but unspectacular racehorse. Justa Bob's love is for an elderly Chinese mother and survivor of the Chinese cultural revolution, who has been every bit as impassive yet dependable as Justa Bob—he thinks of her as Round Pebble (she thinks of him as Iron Plum). Of all the humans he has known, she's the only one he values, and Justa Bob mourns her with a desolate whinny when he is sold and parted from his Round Pebble.

FURY

Part of the popular Saturday morning lineup in the late 1950s, the television show *Fury* tells the story of "Jim," a recent widower and proprietor of the Broken Wheel Ranch, who adopts "Joey," a young city orphan. Jim, who catches and trains wild horses for a living, manages to capture a wild black stallion—named Fury because that's what he's full of. Because of Fury's bronc ways, he is released back to the range, but a heartbroken Joey finds Fury—injured—and saves his life. From then on, only Joey is able to ride the horse. Every Saturday morning for five years, the pair appeared in wild adventures that today's children would surrender their I-Pods for.

Fury was played by a black American Saddlebred horse, Highland Dale, who also had a starring role in *Black Beauty* (1946), *The Gypsy Colt* (1956), and *Grant* (1957).

NATIONAL VELVET

The Pie, Elizabeth Taylor's Grand National steeplechase mount in her star-making movie, *National Velvet* (1944), was played by King Charles, a seven-year-old Thoroughbred gelding, grandson of famous racehorse Man O' War. King Charles, who trained as a show jumper, was a lot to handle. Taylor fell several times, and had compressed vertebrae that contributed to the chronic back pain she experienced in later life. Billy Cartlidge, Taylor's stunt double, was also injured.

In 1960, MGM made a television series based on the movie (Lorie Martin played Velvet Brown; three-year-old colt Blaze King was The Pie). In 1978, Tatum O'Neal starred in *International Velvet,* in which Velvet Brown's niece aspires to be an Olympic equestrian. Mickey Rooney (who played a former jockey Mi Taylor in *National Velvet*) was no stranger to equestrian roles, having appeared as a jockey in *Down the Stretch* (1936) and *Thoroughbreds Don't Cry* (1937), and later as a horse trainer in Francis Ford Coppola's *Black Stallion* (1979).

HORSES IN *THE* LORD OF *THE* RINGS

Horses are crucial characters in *The Lord of the Rings* trilogy. Far more than mere livestock, pets, or means of travel, these horses have lineage, lore, and play fateful roles in the story, just as do the peoples of Middle Earth.

HORSE	RIDER	INSIDE INFORMATION
Arod (or "Swift")	Legolas	Legolas rides bareback and bridleless.
Asfaloth (an Andalusian stallion)	Arwen	Liv Tyler's riding scenes have her riding a fake horse, or using a stunt double, Jane Abbott (who is Asfaloth's owner in real life).
Brego	Aragorn	Brego (who is in the movie but not in the book) is played by Uraeus, a Danish Warmblood, except in the scene when Brego finds a wounded Aragon, when he is played by A horse called Brownie.
Hasfuel	Aragorn	Played by former racehorse Kenny, named for trainer Kenny Brown, neighbor of Mark Todd, New Zealand's Olympic double gold winner in Eventing.
Shadowfax	Gandalf	Played by Andalusian stallion, Blanco. Shadowfax, King of the Mearas, a fabled line of horses, can be ridden only by Gandalf. However, actor Ian McKellen was not a horse person; in several scenes, either stirrups or a rope around Blanco's neck are visible.
Snowmane	King Theoden	Both king and mount died at THE Battle of Pelennor.

SAM SHEPARD'S EQUINE OEUVRE

Sam Shepard, Pulitzer Prize-winning playwright/actor (and Oscar-winning actress Jessica Lange's husband), has been fascinated by horses throughout his almost 40-year career. The horse has turned up in a variety of genres and guises in Shepard's plays, movies, and books:

- *Geography of a Horse Dreamer* (1971), play
- *Simpatico* (1994), play based on some horse-racing skullduggery perpetrated by two old friends
- *Kicking a Dead Horse* (2007), play first staged at Dublin's Abbey Theatre
- *All the Pretty Horses* (2004), movie, starring Shepard, that is based on Cormac McCarthy's novel
- *Ruffian* (2007), movie directed by Shepard, about the racing mare and tragic heroine, Ruffian; Shepard also stars as her trainer, Frank Whitely
- *Remedy Man* (2002), short story about a horse breaker in his fiction collection, *Great Dream of Heaven*.

THE NOTORIOUS BELLE

Belle Starr ran a Dallas livery barn where she sold horses stolen by her husband, Jim Reed of the Cole Younger/Jesse James gangs. In 1880, Reed was killed in Paris, Texas. Belle then married Sam Starr, and the newlyweds opened a new, improved horse-stealing business. Arrested several times for horse stealing, the notorious Belle became known as the Bandit Queen. In 1886, on yet another stealing horses charge, Belle showed her "boss mare" attitude by defending herself and winning an acquittal.

When Belle died (shot off a horse), her daughter Pearl hired a stone cutter to create a memorial, which was topped by a statue of Belle's favorite—and, of course, stolen—horse, Venus.

THE GOLDEN HORSE MONASTERY

The Golden Horse Monastery is set in the jungly, mountainous region near Thailand's border with Myanmar (formerly Burma), a center of the opium and heroin trade. (Thailand has one of the highest drug addiction rates in the world.) Here, a visitor might encounter ponies ridden bareback over the rough trails by barefooted boys wearing the saffron robes of Buddhist monks. Although this seems like a scene from an ancient story, the young monks and their ponies are on a very modern mission—to bring aid to the drug addicts that are common in the country's remote villages.

The monastery was founded by Abbot Khru Ba Nua Cha, a former boxer, now called Tiger Monk. More than 100 horses are kept there, and each boy is responsible for his own horse. Learning to care for and ride horses teaches the boys toughness and self-reliance, qualities that Tiger Monk feels are necessary in their harsh surroundings. The boy monks are orphans, or children of poor local families, and their parents are often casualties of the region's drug culture.

THE YEAR OF THE HORSE

In the Chinese zodiac, a horse is one of the 12-year cycles of animals. It is free-spirited, intelligent, and creative. Check the list to see if you're a HORSE.

- Jan. 25, 1906–Feb. 2, 1907   Fire Horse
- Feb. 11, 1918–Jan. 31, 1919   Earth Horse
- Jan. 30, 1930–Feb. 6, 1931   Metal Horse
- Feb. 15, 1942–Feb. 4, 1943   Water Horse
- Feb. 3, 1954–Feb. 6, 1955   Wood Horse
- Jan. 21, 1966–Feb. 8, 1967   Fire Horse
- Feb. 7, 1978–Jan. 27, 1979   Earth Horse
- Jan. 27, 1990–Feb. 14, 1991   Metal Horse
- Feb. 12, 2002–Jan. 31, 2003   Water Horse
- 2014–2015   Wood Horse
- 2026–2027   Fire Horse

DEGAS'S HORSES

The French painter and sculptor Edward Degas (1834–1917) found in the horse one of his most enduring and intriguing subjects. Degas produced at least 90 paintings of racehorses and 150 equine sculptures in wax and bronze. He even wrote a sonnet about horses, in which he describes them as strong, sound, and precocious.

Degas's equine sculptures—of horses unridden and unadorned—reveal his curiosity about the horse and celebrate their movement. (He is also well-known as a painter and sculptor of dancers.) Degas was an habitué of the Longchamps racetrack outside Paris, where he also made studies of the grooms. He once remarked playfully to a friend, "I have not yet made enough horses . . . the women must wait in their basins." (He also painted women bathers.)

"Two Horses in a Meadow" (1871) is a slightly atypical, but very lovely, horse painting by Degas. It shows two substantial farming horses standing quietly in a field, a dark bay resting his head across the withers of a gray horse, whose large rump is turned to the viewer. The painting exquisitely captures a moment of quiet affection between two horses, away from people and at peace.

WILLIAM FAULKNER

Nobel Prize-winning author William Faulkner (1897–1962), or "Count No Count" to his southern neighbors, was known as a poor rider, but still a devoted and determined one. Not long before his death, he took a bad fall from his horse Tempy. Faulkner enjoyed the rich Southern traditions surrounding the cult of the horse; he belonged to a hunt club and hunted up to the last year of his life, and he was photographed several times in full hunting regalia.

Faulkner claimed that he wrote his most commercial novel, *Sanctuary* (1931), for money: "I needed it to buy a good horse." His equine short stories include "Fool About A Horse," "Notes On A Horse Thief," "Fox Hunt," "Mule In the Yard," "Spotted Horses," and "Race At Morning."

HORSES IN SONG

Horses are such familiar companions and universal symbols, appealing to humans on so many levels, it is little surprise they've found their way into so many iconic songs of the twentieth century. Here's a sampling of songs about horses, with a few notes about the most memorable:

Tennessee Stud—written by Jimmie Driftwood, covered by Eddie Arnold, Johnny Cash, Doc Watson & the Nitty Gritty Dirt Band, the Osborne Brothers, The Chieftains, The Little Willies, and Arlo Guthrie. The ballad tells of a dual human/equine romance. A lover escapes from Arkansas, fleeing his sweetheart's angry family: "I never would have made it through the Arkansas mud, if I hadn't been ridin' on the Tennessee Stud." After various adventures, abetted by his horse, the rider eventually makes it back to Arkansas, where he whups his enemies and wins his sweetheart with golden hair who rides the Tennessee Mare. At the ballad's end, both a child and a colt play by the door of the lovers, who have been reunited thanks to the Tennessee Stud and the Tennessee Mare.

Wild Horses—The Rolling Stones. Conflicting legends abound concerning which Rolling Stone lady inspired this beautiful song. Jerry Hall has called it her favorite, claiming it was so beautiful that she didn't care if it was about Bianca. Marianne Faithfull said the song's refrain "Wild horses couldn't drag me away" was something she murmured to Mick when she regained consciousness after a drug-induced coma. There are also claims that Keith Richards wrote it because he didn't want to leave his young son, Marlon, to go on tour. Meanwhile, Mick has enigmatically conceded, "I was definitely very inside this song emotionally."

Horse Latitudes—Jim Morrison with The Doors. Morrison wrote this song in high school, after seeing a book cover showing horses being thrown overboard from a ship, an image he found compelling. His song is a poetic invocation of the tale of the horse latitudes, which, located at both 30 degrees north and south of the equator, form a subtropical high, with weak winds caused by high pressure and subsiding dry air. When Spanish vessels carrying Iberian horses to the New World became stuck in these eerie pockets of muggy heat, sailors lightened the load by throwing horses overboard. In a 1968 interview, Morrison noted that the horses could swim for a little while, but were no match for the open sea, and they would slowly sink away.

SONG TITLE	PERFORMED BY
All the Pretty L'il Horses	Shawn Colvin
Back in the Saddle Again	Aerosmith
Big Belly Horse	The Ethiopians
Chestnut Mare	Roger McGuinn (The Byrds)
Horse With No Name	America
Horses (The Album)	Patti Smith
Horses in My Dreams	P .J. Harvey
Horses in the City	Nina Gordon
Mollie and Tenbrooks	Ian & Sylvia
The Pony Man	Gordon Lightfoot
Run for the Roses	Dan Fogelberg
Skewball	Traditional
The Strawberry Roan	Curley Fletcher
Two White Horses	John Lee Hooker
Where the Ponies Come to Drink	Poem by Henry Herbert Nibbs; Music by Ed Stabler
Who's Gonna Ride Your Wild Horses?	U2
Why Do Girls Love Horses?	Adam Ant
Wildfire	Michael Murphy

TWO MEN IN A HORSE

A staple of vaudeville acts and British pantomimes, a horse suit is usually worn by two actors. One plays the front end of the horse, standing upright and operating the head and the front legs. The second actor bends over and places their arms around the waist of their partner, so that their own back forms the back of the horse, while their legs become the hind legs.

Playing the back end of the horse is considered by far the less desirable part. Not only does the actor have to perform in a very uncomfortable posture, but it is also much harder to see—and to breathe.

THE TOLSTOYS
AND THEIR HORSES

Few writers have written of the horse with as much detail and true sympathy as the nineteenth-century Russian novelist, Count Leo Tolstoy (1828–1910). As a nobleman, estate owner, and cavalry soldier, he was able to observe horses in all their traditional and societal roles. His novels and short stories are richly supplied with equine vignettes. His short story "Strider" is told in the voice of an ancient piebald horse, ridden by an old peasant tending a herd of mares and foals in a meadow. The horse recounts the story of his life to the foals and yearlings, but there is no happy ending—his owner decides the piebald's time has come. His throat is cut, his hide tanned, and his carcass left for the wolves.

Tolstoy's great-great niece Alexandra leads horse treks into the mountains of Kyrgyzstan, and *The Last Secrets of the Silk Road* (2003) descries her eight-month journey by horseback along this famous trading route.

RITA MAE BROWN

Rita Mae Brown, prolific author of over 32 novels and screenplays, raises and trains foxhunters. She founded the Blue Ridge Polo Club (the United States' only all-female polo club) and is also master of the Oak Ridge Foxhunt in Virginia. Brown's horse passion was inherited from her mother, who had an excellent eye for a horse, a detailed knowledge of bloodlines, and made her "pin" money at the track—often with Rita Mae in tow.

Brown created two mystery series with equine themes—the "Sister Jane" (about a fictional Jefferson Hunt in Virginia Horse country) and "Mrs. Murphy" mysteries (co-authored with her tiger cat, Mrs. Murphy!).

In addition, Brown has written *Riding Shotgun,* a time-travel novel with an equine theme, in which the heroine Cig and her horse, Full Throttle, follow a mysterious fox called Fattail into Virginia's seventeenth-century colonial past.

LITERARY HORSES

AUTHOR	NOVEL
Carolyn Banks	*Dressage mysteries*
Jilly Cooper	Romantic novels: *Polo* and *Riders*
Barbara Dimmick	*In the Presence of Horses*
Nicholas Evans	*The Horse Whisperer*
Dick Francis	Racing thrillers, including *Wild Horses*
Rumer Godden	*The Dark Horse* and other titles
Aryn Kyle	*The God of Animals*
Cormac McCarthy	*All the Pretty Horses*
Laura Moore	*Ride a Dark Horse*
Mary O'Hara	*My Friend Flicka, Thunderhead* (son of Flicka), and *Green Grass of Wyoming*
Mary Oldham	*The White Pony*
Katherine Anne Porter	*Pale Horse, Pale Rider*
Jane Smiley	*Horse Heaven*
Danielle Steel	*Palomino*
John Steinbeck	*The Red Pony*
Mary Stewart	*Airs Above the Ground* (about a lost Lipizzan)

LINDA MCCARTNEY

Linda McCartney's devotion to horses and riding is evident from the fact that shortly before her death from cancer in 1998, she retreated to Arizona, with husband Paul, to ride. Blankit, her Appaloosa stallion, was bred on the McCartney farm. Linda also wrote the lyrics for "Appaloosa" (about the history of the breed with the Nez Percé tribe along Oregon's Palouse River), which was on the posthumously released album, "Wide Prairie" (1998).

Paul honored Linda's devotion to the breed by having Pay N' Go (a 16.2-hand, leopard-spot Appaloosa stallion) perform a Spanish Walk at her memorial service in Manhattan. Paul also led Schoo and Tinsel (Linda's Shetland ponies) up the aisle of St. Martin-in-the-Fields Church at her London memorial service.

Stella McCartney remembered her mother by hanging a chandelier—designed as a 10-foot (3-m)-tall rearing horse, made of 3,000 Swarovski crystals—from the rafters of the fourteenth-century Belsay Castle in northern England. Linda once said, "I would travel only by horse, if I had my choice."

A SURVIVOR'S TALE

Comanche, a 15-hand Bay gelding (of Mustang and Morgan ancestry), was apparently the sole survivor of The Battle of Little Bighorn (also known as Custer's Last Stand—or The Battle of the Greasy Grass, to Native Americans). Discovered two days after the battle, wounded and so weak that he could not stand, Comanche was transferred to Fort Lincoln via steamboat and nursed back to health, with orders that he never be ridden again. After his recovery, Comanche was stabled at Fort Riley, and was trotted out for parades and an appearance at the 1893 World's Fair in Chicago.

He lived to 29—possibly aided by regular infusions of beer, which soldiers discovered was his favorite drink! When Comanche died, his body was sent to the University of Kansas Museum of Natural History, where a taxidermist did his thing. However, the soldiers never retrieved Comanche, so to this day he resides, stuffed, in a glass case at the museum.

MADONNA'S FALL

Madonna can't even fall off her horse without being analyzed! She was seriously injured on her 47th birthday when she fell from a polo pony at her Ashecombe estate, breaking her hand, collarbone, and cracking several ribs.

The literary and cultural critic Camille Paglia, who has praised Madonna in the past, accused her of using horses as fashion accessories—warning the famously disciplined singer that even her legendary will would not automatically transform her into a skillful rider, as riding requires "self-subordination."

SPOTLESS STABLES

Martha Stewart hosted Thanksgiving Dinner 2006 in her very clean horse barn. Her perfectly groomed Friesian horses were graciously fed home-grown carrots, with green tops attached, by the assembled guests.

Her rival for swankiest and most spotless horse operation might be Ralph Lauren, at his Double RL (for Ralph & Ricky Lauren) Horse Ranch in Colorado.

WILLIE NELSON

Country music legend Willie Nelson campaigns in support of the American Horse Slaughter Prevention Act—which would ban horse slaughter in the United States and the export of live horses for slaughter abroad. He has also adopted many horses from Habitat for Horses, an equine rescue organization.

HAIRY HORSES

Comedian Chevy Chase keeps Icelandic horses—and he once noted:
"They get very hairy in the winter, but then, so do I."

ELVIS AND HIS HORSES

Elvis, a true Southerner, was a fan of Tennessee Walking Horses. Ebony's Double was a black Tennessee Walker, who first caught Elvis's eye because he was wearing bright red leg wraps. Elvis found the combination so striking that he purchased the horse. Unfortunately, Ebony's Double was delivered without the legs wraps, leaving his new owner in doubt as to whether he was the same horse. Fortunately, the leg wraps were restored and the stallion stayed at Graceland all his life, passing away at the age of 32 in 2005.

At one time or another, there were up to 20 horses at Graceland, including Memphis (another Tennessee Walker), Moriah (Lisa Marie's Shetland pony), Rising Sun (Elvis's favorite Palomino Quarter Horse), and Mare Ingram, a grade (unregistered horse)—who Elvis named, in a humorous turnabout, after Mayor Bill Ingram of Memphis (who had christened Elvis Presley Boulevard there).

It was said—and photographs prove it—that Elvis was a good rider, with a natural sense of rhythm and good hands.

There is something about the outside of a horse that is good for the inside of a man.
WINSTON CHURCHILL (1874–1965), STATESMAN

THE HORSE WHO WAS A ROMAN CONSUL

Incitatus was the favored horse of Roman emperor Caligula (A.D. 12–41), who can easily be described as being mad. According to the historian Suetonius (A.D. *c.*69–*c.*140), Incitatus was attended by 18 servants, ate oats mixed with gold flake, had an ivory manger, horse blankets of imperial purple, a collar of precious stones, and a "wife" named Penelope. Caligula also admitted Incitatus to the priesthood and appointed him a Roman consul!

ROYAL RIDING INJURIES

It was the famous Elizabethan poet and dramatist Ben Jonson (1572–1637), a contemporary of Shakespeare, who once wrote:

"They say princes learn no art truly, but the art of horsemanship. The reason is, the brave beast is no flatterer. He will throw a prince as soon as his groom."

Prince Charles can only agree with this maxim. Although he retired from polo in 2005, at the age of 57, over the years His Royal Highness has acquired an impressive resumé of "brave beast"-related injuries.

〇 1980: Collapsed after a polo match and had to be revived by an IV and internal fluids.

〇 1980: Six stitches in cheek after being thrown; sports rakish cheek scar as a result.

〇 1990: Fell, then was kicked by a disrespectful horse when down. Sustained a broken arm that took two operations to correct.

〇 1992: Surgery to repair knee injury that was sustained during a polo match.

〇 1998: Broken rib after a fall during a foxhunt.

〇 2001: At age 52, knocked unconscious after a fall during another foxhunt, in which the horse tumbled on top of him.

〇 2001: Fractured shoulder during yet another foxhunt.

QUEEN ELIZABETH II

In July 1953, Queen Elizabeth II became the first rider in ten years to sit on the back of the Lipizzan stallion, Pluto Theodorosta, besides Alois Podhajsky (its trainer, Olympic medalist, and director of Vienna's Spanish Riding School). After seeing a performance of the latter in London, Her Majesty showed intense interest in the Lipizzans, impressing Podhajsky with her detailed knowledge of the school's history and its traditional dressage training methods. Later, in a private lesson, the Queen not only rode the exquisitely sensitive stallion in the trot and canter but also, according to Podhajsky, was able to perform (with his coaching help) the difficult movements of piaffe and passage.

Eight years later, Jacqueline Kennedy (whose girlhood horse was a chestnut mare named Danseuse) approached Podhajsky at a reception and asked if she, too, could ride a Lipizzan. She repeated her request with a handwritten note, but it never came to pass. Like the Queen, she was an experienced, passionate rider.

MORE ROYAL RIDERS

Granddaughter of Queen Elizabeth II, Zara Phillips won the 2005 European Eventing and 2006 World Eventing championships on her horse Toytown, and will represent Great Britain in the 2008 Beijing Olympics. She follows the example of her mother, Princess Anne, and father, Captain Mark Phillips.

Princess Anne won the European Eventing championship, with her horse Doublet, at the 1971 Burghley Horse Trials, and rode for the British eventing team at the 1976 Montreal Olympics. Her Royal Highness also won individual and team silver medals at the 1975 European Eventing Championships.

Zara's father, Mark Phillips (divorced from Princess Anne since 1992), is one of the most sought-after eventing trainers in the world. Trainer of the U.S. eventing team since 1993, he is a four-time winner of the Badminton Horse Trials, and won team gold and silver medals at the Munich (1972) and Seoul (1988) Olympics. Phillips' second wife, Sandy Pflueger-Phillips, a competitor in dressage at the 1984 Los Angeles Olympics, is one of Zara's coaches in dressage.

KATHY KUSNER

Like many famous equestrians, Kusner passes on her joy of horses by teaching riding and horse care. This unique horsewoman's achievements are amazing:
• three Olympics in Tokyo, 1964; Mexico City, 1968; won silver at Munich, 1972
• two Pan American Games in Sao Paulo, 1963, and Winnipeg, 1967
• twice leading rider at Madison Square Garden
• two-time winner of Grand Prix in Dublin; puissance (high jumps) in Germany
• winner of Grand Prix in France, Netherlands, Belgium, Germany, Switzerland
• first woman to ride in the prestigious Maryland Hunt Cup (steeplechase).

In 1968, Kusner won the right to become the first licensed female jockey in the United States. She is also a licensed pilot, and has completed 105 marathons and 66 ultramarathons. She is a member of the Show Jumping Hall of Fame, and has been named by *The Chronicle of the Horse* as one of the 50 most influential horsepeople of the century. In 1992, Kusner opened Horses in The Hood in Watts, Los Angeles, where, to date, more than 500 at-risk, inner-city children have learned to ride.

ATHENA ROUSSEL

Granddaughter of the Greek shipping tycoon Aristotle Onassis (husband of Jackie O) and one of the world's richest young women, Athina Roussel is a talented show jumper. She is married to Brazilian show jumper Álvaro Miranda Neto, a two-time Olympic medalist. The couple live in Brazil, where Athina trains with the goal of riding for Greece's Olympic show jumping team.

WILLIAM SHATNER

William Shatner—or Captain Kirk, as he is known to legions of *Star Trek* fans—is an enthusiast of the Quarter Horse and American Saddlebred breeds. Shatner breeds Quarter Horses, owns a world champion Saddlebred (Sultan's Great Day), and also won the 1997 World Harness Championships with another Saddlebred (Revival).

BEAUTIFUL JIM KEY

From 1897–1906, the United States was in love with Beautiful Jim Key, offspring of an Arab mare (once owned by P. T. Barnum) and a Standardbred stallion. Jim's breeder and owner, William Key, was a former Tennessee slave and self-taught veterinarian who had a gentle way with horses. "Dr." Key handraised the sickly foal Jim, who developed into a strong, smart horse. Key first noticed that Jim was unusual when the horse began to imitate the actions of a dog—picking up sticks, dropping them for Key to throw, then bringing them back again. Dr. Key began to work with Jim, developing his intelligence, so that he could allegedly pick letters out of a deck of cards to spell words and answer questions, do math, sort mail, tell time, identify colors, even answer questions about politics.

STAR ATTRACTION

Jim became a phenomenon. He met President McKinley and Alice Roosevelt. Indeed, he was so popular that children were given a school holiday when he came to town, solemnly taking the "Beautiful Big Jim Key Pledge" to be kind to animals. The banner headline on flyers extolling Jim was: "He was trained with kindness." Jim and Dr. Key are credited with popularizing the American Humane Society movement. Jim's own souvenir line included buttons, postcards, statues, pennies, and pamphlets. He was also the star attraction at the 1904 St. Louis World's Fair.

AN INCREDIBLE LIFE

Dr. Key was a fascinating man in his own right. Because of his loyalty to the family who had "owned" him, he fought for the Confederates in the Civil War, yet he secretly helped slaves escape via the underground railroad. He was caught and sentenced to be hanged, but his skill as a poker player entranced his captors and he was freed. After the war, Dr. Key went back to his former owners' ruined farm, where his veterinarian skills were in demand. He concocted and successfully marketed a homemade horse liniment, which enabled him to buy the farm of his former owners and support the family. Dr. Key died at age 76; Jim, part of the Key family, passed away three years later.

CLEVER HANS

An Arab stallion owned by high school teacher Wilhelm von Osten, Clever Hans gained enormous fame in Germany in the early years of the twentieth century by displaying feats of intelligence never before seen in a horse.

To the amazement of onlookers, Hans displayed the ability to add, subtract, multiply, and divide, and to solve both written and verbal math problems by tapping out the correct answer with his hoof. Hans was also supposedly able to tell the time and understand German.

HOAX OR NO HOAX?

Suspecting a hoax, a panel of scientists (the Hans Commission) conducted a series of tests, but they were amazed when Hans passed with flying colors. The eggheads were baffled until psychologist Oskar Pfungst came up with a new theory.

Pfungst believed that the body language of the questioner was giving Hans clues. When Hans began to tap out an answer, the questioner would involuntarily tense up, only to relax when Hans reached the correct number of taps. Hans would notice this almost imperceptible change and stop tapping, thereby seeming to solve the problem.

To test this theory, Pfungst used a clever test. One of his team wrote a sum on a blackboard, then left the room. Pfungst, standing where he could not see the blackboard, then asked Hans to solve the problem. As Pfungst himself did not know what the correct answer was, he obviously couldn't supply any subconscious cues. And without that assistance, "Clever" Hans was stumped!

> *"Thou must learn the thoughts of the noble horse whom thou wouldst ride. Be not indiscreet in thy demands, nor require him to perform indiscreetly."*
>
> JOHANN W. VON GOETHE (1749–1832), GERMAN POET

A HORSE IN THE WHITE HOUSE

From transporting people and goods to providing recreation for presidents and their families, horses played an important and varied role in the early history of the White House. Many early presidents formed lifetime bonds with their wartime mounts, for example George Washington and his horse Nelson. After the Civil War, horses were used to project an image of heroism and leadership, and many presidents around this time feature with their horses in equestrian art. Horseracing was a popular sport in the nineteenth century, and Thomas Jefferson and Andrew Jackson had a keen interest in racing horses. Andrew Jackson, a notorious gambler who once fought a duel over a bet on a horse, even bred racehorses from a stable on the White House grounds.

PRESIDENTS' FAVORITE HORSES

PRESIDENT	FAVORITE HORSE
George Washington	Nelson
John Adams	Cleopatra
Andrew Jackson	Sam Patches (warhorse)
	Truxton (racehorse)
John Tyler	The General
Zachary Taylor	Old Whitey
Ulysses S. Grant	Cincinnati
Theodore Roosevelt	Bleistein
Ronald Reagan	El Alamein

PONIES OF PRESIDENTS' CHILDREN

CHILD	PONY
Caroline Kennedy	Macaroni and Tex
John Kennedy Jr.	Leprechaun
Quentin Roosevelt	Algonquin
Tad Lincoln	unknown names

WHITE HOUSE HORSE ANECDOTES

🐎 Quentin Roosevelt took his calico pony, Algonquin, up in the elevator to brother Archie's bedroom to cheer him up when he was sick with the measles.

🐎 In the time of Zachary Taylor, visitors to the White House would pluck hairs from the tail of his horse, Old Whitey, for luck.

🐎 John Tyler buried his horse, The General, with a headstone reading "Here lies the body of my good horse, 'The General.' For twenty years he bore me around the circuit of my practice, and in all that time he never made a blunder. Would that his master could say the same! John Tyler."

THE RIDERLESS HORSE

A riderless horse takes part in U.S. military funeral processions. The horse wears full regalia, including an artillery sword, and walks behind a caisson bearing the casket. A pair of empty boots are reversed in its stirrups to symbolize a fallen leader. The honor is accorded to high-ranking army officers, and to former presidents in accordance with their position as commander in chief of the U.S. army. The most famous riderless horse in American History is Black Jack, named for General John J. (Black Jack) Pershing. During Black Jack's military career (1953–73), he served as a "caparisoned" (riderless) horse for the state funerals of Herbert Hoover, John F. Kennedy, and Lyndon B. Johnson. Another famous riderless horse is Sergeant York, a racehorse formerly known as Allaboard Jules, who was donated to the U.S. army in 1997. Sergeant York served as the riderless horse for President Reagan's funeral in 2004.

CHAPTER 3

Horse Sports

....

Is there anything that an equine athlete cannot do? From the

balletic movements of dressage to the rough-and-tumble of polo and

bushkazi, from the derring-do of puissance jumps to the nimble

responsiveness of the cutting horse, horses show a genius for athletics

that can thrill a stadium. The finest horses can induce the wealthy

to part company with millions of dollars in hopes of owning or

breeding a noble champion. The marvelous equine body that

performs such feats, however, is also delicate—an inescapable fact

that has led over the years to some terrible tragedies.

KENTUCKY AND EPSOM DERBY WINNERS

YEAR	KENTUCKY	EPSOM
1971	Canonero II	Mill Reef
1972	Riva Ridge	Roberto
1973	Secretariat	Morston
1974	Cannonade	Snow Knight
1975	Foolish Pleasure	Grundy
1976	Bold Forbes	Empery
1977	Seattle Slew	The Minstrel
1978	Affirmed	Shirley Heights
1979	Spectacular Bid	Troy
1980	Genuine Risk	Henbit
1981	Pleasant Colony	Shergar
1982	Gato Del Sol	Golden Fleece
1983	Sunny's Halo	Teenoso
1984	Swale	Secreto
1985	Spend A Buck	Slip Anchor
1986	Ferdinand	Shahranstani
1987	Alysheba	Reference Point
1988	Winning Colors	Kahyasi
1989	Sunday Silence	Nashwan
1990	Unbridled	Quest for Fame
1991	Strike The Gold	Generous
1992	Lil E Tee	Dr. Devious
1993	Sea Hero	Commander in Chief
1994	Go For Gin	Erhaab
1995	Thunder Gulch	Lammtarra
1996	Grindstone	Shaamit
1997	Silver Charm	Benny the Dip
1998	Real Quiet	High-Rise
1999	Charismatic	Oath
2000	Fusaichi Pegasus	Sinndar
2001	Monarchos	Galileo
2002	War Emblem	High Chaparral
2003	Funny Cide	Kris Kin
2004	Smarty Jones	North Light
2005	Giacomo	Motivator
2006	Barbaro	Sir Percy
2007	Street Sense	Authorized

ALL-TIME PRIZE-WINNING JOCKEYS

JOCKEY/PLACE OF BIRTH	WINS	EARNINGS
Pat Day/Colorado	8,803	$297,912,019
Jerry Bailey/Texas	5,893	$296,104,129
Chris McCarron/Massachusetts	7,141	$263,985,505
Laffit Pincay, Jr./Panama	9,530	$237,120,625
Gary Stevens/Idaho	4,888	$221,207,064
Alex Solis/Panama	4,516	$204,509,847
Edgar Prado/Peru	5,952	$199,566,285
Kent Desormeaux/Louisiana	4,846	$196,374,214
Eddie Delahoussaye/Louisiana	6,384	$195,884,940
John Velazquez/Puerto Rico	3,786	$191,804,229

THE CALIFORNIA COMET

Silky Sullivan, "The California Comet," was a racehorse who didn't always win, but often he was more popular than the winners. He transfixed the public with his unorthodox racing style. "And here comes Silky Sullivan!" became a familiar and much-loved cry during his racing days.

WHAT A HAM!

Silky was a ham. He'd break out of the gate, but after a few lengths he slowed to a measured lope—later turning on the famous Silky Sullivan stretch run! His owner, Phil Klipstein, who had heart trouble, was forbidden to watch Silky's nerve-racking races. Legendary Bill Shoemaker was Silky's jockey, but all his skill could never persuade Silky to pick up the pace early on.

As a two year old, Silky came from 27 lengths behind to win the Golden Gate Futurity. In the Santa Anita Derby, he was 28 lengths behind, then won by 3½ lengths. His stretch run for the record books came in 1958, when he came from a flabbergasting 41 lengths behind to win a 6½ furlong allowance race!

In the 1958 Kentucky Derby, CBS had a split screen to keep an eye on Silky's "Run for the Roses." Knowing he would be far off the pace, the rest of the field got the big screen while Silky had a special "cam" to himself. But that day, Silky, who hated mud, would not oblige with one of his signature 20-second closing quarter miles. Silky was fussy about his racing conditions.

A BATTLESHIP UNDER ESCORT

Silky's stretch runs were fueled by his powerful build. At his birth it was noted that Silky had the biggest rear end seen on a foal. William Robertson, writing in *The History of Thoroughbred Racing in America*, said: "In a field of typical Thoroughbreds mincing to the post, Silky resembled a battleship under escort." Silky even contributed to the American lexicon—"Doing a Silky Sullivan" became slang for any athlete or politician who came from behind to win.

MARIAH'S STORM

Mariah's Storm showed early promise, winning the Arlington Washington Lassie, a grade 2 stakes race for two-year-old fillies. While prepping for the 1993 Breeder's Cup race (she was the favorite), she fractured her left front cannon bone in Kentucky's Alcibiades Stakes. She was one of the few racehorses ever known to recover from a break and go on to race again—and win!

In August 1994, after a full recovery, she won the Arlington Heights Oaks, a grade 3 stakes for 3-year-old fillies. In September 1995, she won the Arlington Matron Handicap for 3-year-old and older females, becoming the only horse ever to win all three stakes races for her age at Arlington. Arlington Park named a race the Mariah's Storm Stakes in her honor. As a broodmare, Mariah's Storm foaled several champions, including Giant's Causeway, 2000 Horse of the Year and sire of Noble Causeway, who ran in the 2005 Kentucky Derby.

The 2005 movie *Dreamer*, starring Kurt Russell and Dakota Fanning, is loosely based on the story of Mariah's Storm.

RACETRACK ENGINEERING

In 1994, the racing industry asked Michael Peterson, professor of Mechanical Engineering, University of Maine, to investigate the effect of track surfaces on joint loading and stress placed on racehorses' legs. Peterson found deviations not only from track to track but also in different areas of the same track. For example, on one stretch, he found poor drainage had caused a washout 8 inches (20 cm) below the surface, making the track much softer. Such deviations can cause a sudden, tragic end to a racehorse's career. Peterson is calling for standard maintenance protocols that also take into account the effect of temperature and rainfall on the tracks. Race-course managers are also experimenting with new high-tech surfaces such as "polytrack"—a combination of silica, sand, fibers, recycled rubber, and wax.

TRAVERS STAKES

The Travers Stakes, or "Midsummer Derby," inaugurated in 1864 at Saratoga Race Course in Saratoga, New York, is the oldest major Thoroughbred race in the United States. The race was won by Man O' War in 1920, and the Travers Trophy is now known as the "Man O' War Cup."

THE GRAND NATIONAL

Arguably the biggest ever event in the British racing calendar, the Grand National is a handicap chase run over a distance of 4 miles (6.5 km), 4 furlongs, at the Aintree Racecourse near Liverpool. First run in 1839, this grueling race features 30 fences, including the notorious Becher's Brook. Despite protests about the number of horses killed during the race, the Grand National remains popular, with millions of pounds wagered each year. Famous winners have included Red Rum (who won three times) and Mr. Frisk, whose winning time of 8 minutes 47 seconds in 1990, is the fastest in Grand National history.

HOW THE DERBY GOT ITS NAME

It had nothing to do with a hat! By tradition, a "derby" is a race for three year olds, and the term was first used in England in 1779. Edward Smith-Stanley, 12th Earl of Derby, was celebrating the inaugural run of the Epsom Oaks (named after his estate "The Oaks"), which his horse, Bridget, had won.

Derby and his friend Sir Charles Bunbury decided to hold a similar race for three-year-old colts the following year, and the name of the race was decided by a coin toss that went Derby's way. But for a flip of the coin, perhaps we would be celebrating the Kentucky Bunbury every year, on the first Saturday in May! The Epsom Derby was run for the first time in 1780—won, as luck would have it, by Bunbury's colt Diomedes.

THE CLUB-FOOTED COMET

The 1946 Triple Crown winner, Assault, was bred on Texas' fabled King Ranch, far better known for its foundation-bred Quarter Horses than for Thoroughbreds. Nevertheless, the King Ranch had brought some Thoroughbreds into its Quarter Horse breeding program, and one of them, Bold Venture, sired Assault—to this day the only Texas-bred Triple Crown winner.

Assault was called the "Club-footed Comet" because he had a deformed foot—in an accident, a surveyor's stake had cut through his right front foot. Most of the hoof had to be cut away, and Assault had to wear a special shoe. Although he limped at the walk and trot, his limp disappeared at the gallop.

His lifetime record included 18 victories, and his winnings totaled more than $600,000 in the 1940s. After he retired, he was put to stud, but his breedings with other Thoroughbreds were not successful. However, he did sire two foals out of Quarter Horse mares, which were registered with the American Quarter Horse Association.

THE TRIPLE CROWN

The United States is not the only country to have a prestigious series of flat races for three year olds (called the Triple Crown). England inaugurated the term "Triple Crown," in 1853, with a series of races comprised of the Two Thousand Guineas (1 mile/1.5 km, run at Newmarket), the Epsom Derby (1½ mile/2.4 km, run at Epsom Downs), and the St. Leger Stakes (1 mile/1.5 km, 6 furlongs, and 132 yards/120 m, run at Town Moor, Doncaster, Yorkshire).

The United States first ran a series of races (consisting of the Belmont, the Kentucky Derby, and the Preakness) in 1919, but it was not until 1930—when Gallant Fox won all three titles—that the influential sportswriter Charles Hatton began applying the term Triple Crown. Ireland, Canada, Japan, and Hong Kong have also inaugurated Triple Crown race series.

SNOWMAN'S STORY

Did Snowman resolve always to do his best that snowy February day in 1956 when he was pulled from the mass of unwanted horses on their way to the canners? His classic Cinderella story might seem to suggest that he did.

Harry de Leyer, a riding teacher from Long Island looking for a safe school mount, was at an auction of last-chance horses when he noticed the intelligent expression of the raw-boned gray gelding and bought him for $80. When he brought his rescue home it was snowing, so his children named him Snowman.

De Leyer realized the horse had jumping talent (because Snowman kept jumping out of his paddock) and started showing the horse at small shows. Snowman must have been very grateful to Harry, for he became one of the top U.S. show jumpers from 1959 to 1962, winning many national championships.

MGM studios got word of Snowman and, thinking to make a movie, sent the horse to Europe, where he won a puissance class, jumping 7 feet 2 inches (2.2 m). The movie was never made, but Snowman did appear on the cover of *Life* magazine with Marilyn Monroe.

Through it all, Snowman maintained a family-horse temperament, once winning a lead line class (usually for small children and their ponies) and an open jumper championship on the same day. DeLeyer was offered many times the $80 purchase price for the horse, but he would not sell, and Snowman stayed in the de Leyer family until his death at 28. In 1992, he was inducted into the Show Jumping Hall of Fame.

THE BARBAROUS BATTALION

Five full Thoroughbred sisters—Remorseless, Relentless, Regardless, Ruthless, and Merciless—made up the Barbarous Battalion. All five daughters of the mare Barbarity and the fabled sire Eclipse became racing champions. The formidable Ruthless won the 1867 inaugural running of New York's Belmont Stakes (a Triple Crown race). In her 11 starts, Ruthless had 7 wins and 4 seconds. She was inducted into the Racing Hall of Fame in 1975.

A STEEPLECHASER'S SOFA

Steeplechase jockey Tom Olliver gave new meaning to the concept of couch potato by having a sofa made from the hide of his favorite 1843 Grand National winning mount, Vanguard. Despite spending some unscheduled down time in debtor's prison, Olliver managed to ride in a record 18 Grand Nationals, with a final tally of 3 wins, 3 seconds, and 1 third. He was also the first jockey to win two Grand Nationals in a row—Gay Lad (1842), then Vanguard (1843).

> *Men are better when riding, more just and more understanding, and more alert and more at ease and more under-taking, and better knowing of all countries and all passages; in short and long all good customs and manners cometh thereof, and the health of man and of his soul.*
>
> ATTRIBUTED TO EDWARD PLANTAGENET, ENGLISH KING

CREATING A STORM

Stuck in traffic on the way to the horse show? Did your horse have a difficult trailer trip? That's no excuse not to win!

Consider that, in 1904, the New Zealand-bred horse Moiffa won England's grueling Grand National steeplechase—despite having been inconvenienced by a shipwreck that forced him to swim 50 miles (80 km) to the safety of a tiny rocky outcrop off the south coast of Ireland!

Moiffa's owner, New Zealand businessman Spencer Gollan, had shipped him off to the Grand National by sea. A storm kicked up and the boat sank. Luckily, a fisherman heard the horse's neighs of distress and discovered Moiffa on his precarious rocky perch. Proving indisputably that he was a good loader, Moiffa hopped into the boat and found his way to the steeplechase, where—in top condition, despite, or perhaps because of, his swim—he won by 8 lengths.

RAGS TO RICHES

Rags to Riches, the filly who won the 2007 Belmont Stakes in a classic stretch duel (billed by the quick thinking race announcer as "A Battle of the Sexes") was only the third filly to win the Belmont (and the first at the 1½ mile/2.4 km distance). The last filly to win the Belmont was Tanya in 1905.

Rags to Riches overcame a stumble out of the gate, bided her time until the final quarter mile (0.4 km), then showed her scene-stealing power by setting up a match race with Curlin—a perfect showcase for her ability to pull away and prevail at the end, a talent she had previously displayed in her wins of the Santa Anita Derby and Kentucky Oaks.

Rags to Riches comes from an equine family with a tradition of producing Belmont winners. Her grandfather, Seattle Slew, and father, AP Indy, both won the Belmont (in 1977 and 1992, respectively), and her half brother (by the same dam, Better Than Honour), Jazil, won in 2006.

THE BIG APPLE

The "Big Apple," as a name for New York City, was first used by stablehands at the track. In the 1930s, John Fitzgerald was the track columnist for the *New York Morning Telegraph,* covering Belmont, Aqueduct, Jamaica, Empire City Track (now Yonkers Raceway), and Saratoga—his column was titled "Around the Big Apple."

He claimed he heard the term from the stableboys who followed the horses to tracks all over the United States. They loved to come to New York, because there was plenty of money to be made—and as stableboys they were no strangers to apples as rewards, so New York became The Big Apple.

FANCY FOOTWORK

Hungarian cavalry officer Bertalan de Nemethy emigrated to the United States. In 1955, he became the show jumping coach of the U.S. equestrian team. He was a master at the creative use of ground poles (cavalletti) to train the horse. Their advantage is that they make the horse pay attention to where he puts his feet on the ground—"Show your horse the ground" is a time-honored axiom.

Trotting over cavalletti forces the horse to pick up his feet, stretch his neck down—and, therefore, round his back (or bring it "up"), developing the muscles over the back—and helps to regulate the horse's stride.

A CURSE AGAINST THE RIVAL CHARIOT TEAM

Help me in the Circus on November 8. Bind every limb, every sinew, the shoulders, the ankles, and the elbows of Olympus, Olympianus, Scortius, and Juvencus—the charioteers of the Red. Torment their minds, their intelligence, and their senses so that they may not know what they are doing, and knock out their eyes so that they may not see where they are going—neither they nor the horses they are going to drive.

TRANSLATED BY H. A. HARRIS, *SPORT IN GREECE AND ROME*

LITTLE GIANTS

Competition horses are asked to perform such grueling feats that it seems natural to assume that horses of a certain stature (say 16 to 17 hands) would have a natural advantage—but never discount a horse or pony on the basis of height alone. Some of the most outstanding performance horses of the past century have been ponies, or very small horses.

◡ DUNDRUM: 15.1 hands, Connemara. Cleared 7 ft. 2 in. (2.2 m) wall at Wembley (London) Horse of the Year Show. International Jumping Champion (1959–63).

◡ LITTLE SQUIRE: 13.2 hands, Connemara. Winner of 1939 Open Championship at Madison Square Garden horse show, where he cleared a 7 ft. (2.1 m) fence.

◡ THE NUGGET: 15 hands, Connemara gelding. At the age of 22, cleared a 7 ft. 2 in. (2.2 m) jump at the 1935 International Horse Show.

◡ STROLLER: 14.2 hands, Connemara. Only pony to compete in Olympics (Great Britain, in Mexico, 1968), winning a silver individual medal, ridden by owner Marion Coakes Mould.

◡ THEODORE O'CONNOR ("TEDDY"): 14.1 hands. "Bionic pony" Teddy was third at the Rolex 4 star CCI (the first-ever pony to compete in this extremely challenging event), winning team and individual gold medals at the 2007 Pan American Games in Rio de Janeiro.

THE SIZE OF A PONY

No more than 14.2 hands high (hh), a pony is a very small, sturdy horse, and is noted for its gentleness, intelligence, and endurance. Of Celtic origin, all pony breeds now have Thoroughbred and Arab blood (except for the hardy Shetland, which is less than 10.2 hh). Ponies differ from horses—they have thicker manes and tails, shorter legs, wider bodies, heavier bones, thicker necks, and shorter heads.

CALGARY STAMPEDE

The Calgary Stampede is a ten-day rodeo held in Calgary, Alberta, Canada, and is billed as the world's largest outdoor rodeo. First held in 1912, the brainchild of American trick roper Guy Weadick, the Stampede became an invitation-only rodeo event in 2006, with top competitors from other major rodeos and prize money of $1.6 million at stake.

The Stampede has suffered controversy over the years. Although it has adopted many safety measures and conducts yearly safety reviews, animal casualties are not unknown. In 2002, six horses were put down after being injured during the Chuckwagon Races, while in 2005, nine horses died after they jumped off a bridge and drowned during the Trail Ride into the city.

The Stampede also features unusual events, such as wild pony racing, in which teams of children betweeen 8 and 12 years old try to control a wild pony long enough to get in a "two jump" ride. Both ponies and children in this event are said to be some of the most fearsome competitors in the entire Stampede!

A SMALL SUCCESS STORY

Born small and sickly, Hyperion at maturity was only 15.1 hh. He was almost gelded because of his unimpressive stature, but trainer George Lambton took a liking to the colt, noting that his head was full of character and courage.

Hyperion's prestigious wins in 1933 were the Epsom Derby (in a record time of 2 minutes, 34 seconds) and the St. Leger stakes. Hyperion was one of the greatest Thoroughbred racehorse sires ever, with 527 foals, of whom 118 won stakes, including 7 winners of 11 English classics; he was also was the grandsire of the twentieth-century's greatest racehorse sire, Northern Dancer.

Hyperion's skeleton is displayed at the Animal Health Trust, and a lifesize statue stands in front of the Jockey Club offices (both in Newmarket, England).

RODEO EVENTS

In a rodeo competition, there are two categories—roughstock events and timed events, with three competitions each for the two events.

ROUGHSTOCK EVENTS include bareback, saddlebronc, and bull riding. The score for these events is determined by the performance of both rider and animal. The animals are judged on the quality of their "bucking action." All riding must be one handed—if the rider touches any part of the animal or himself with his free hand, he is disqualified.

Bareback Riding: Cowboys ride broncs (rogue horses) without saddle or bridle, with only a leather rigging and a single handle about the size of a briefcase handle. Bareback riders are judged on spurring technique—toes should be turned out, and the rider must spur from the points of the horse's shoulders toward the back of the saddle.

Saddlebronc Riding: Saddlebronc saddles are light with no horn. This event requires more finesse than bareback riding—cowboys try to stay on for 8 seconds and a "fluid" ride is their objective.

Bull Riding: This is undoubtedly the most dangerous event of the rodeo because of the fearsomeness of the 1,500-pound (680-kg) bulls, which the cowboys attempt to ride bareback.

TIMED EVENTS consist of barrel racing, steer wrestling, and team roping. Speed is the crucial factor in these events.

Barrel Racing: Cowgirls race against the clock in a cloverleaf pattern around a series of barrels. Traditionally, barrel racing is a women's event.

Steer Wrestling: The cowboy leaps from his galloping horse, grabs the steer by the horns, and tries to throw the animal to the ground.

Team Roping: A pairs event, in which one cowboy ropes the horn of the steer, while the other tries to lasso its hind legs.

LASSOER IN LINGERIE

Lucille Mulhall (1885–1940), a petite woman with a pixie face, grew up on her family's Oklahoma ranch, where she honed the horseback skills that impressed even Chief Geronimo. He admired Lucille so much that he presented her with a beaded vest and a decorated Indian bow.

Lucille won three gold medals for steer roping at Texas rodeos. Competing against seasoned working cowhands, she won the competition—and $10,000—by lassoing and tying three steers in 3 minutes, 36 seconds. In those pre-politically correct days, newspapermen dubbed her the "Lassoer in Lingerie."

She taught more than 40 tricks to her horse Governor. He could take off a man's coat and put it back on, walk up and down stairs, and sit down with his front legs crossed. When Lucille appeared at Madison Square Garden, Will Rogers invented the term "cowgirl" to describe her. In rodeos and western riding competitions, Lucille took titles, such as World Champion Roper, Queen of the Saddle, and America's Greatest Horsewoman.

When she died at only 55—in a car crash—horses pulled the wagon that carried her to her grave.

WORLD'S OLDEST RODEO

The world's oldest rodeo dates back to July, 1888, in Prescott, Arizona, where it was billed as a "cowboy tournament." The committee organizing the rodeo included Bucky O'Neill, later of Teddy Roosevelt's Rough Riders, and Morris Goldwater, the town mayor and uncle of 1964 Republican presidential candidate, Barry Goldwater—who often participated in the rodeo and once said that it was his secret desire as a child to become a cowboy.

TEVIS ENDURANCE RIDE

Held every year since 1955, the Tevis Endurance Ride covers 100 miles (160 km) in 24 hours through wilderness in the Sierra Nevada Mountains. It starts in Lake Tahoe, California, and ends in Auburn, California—with nearly 17,040 feet (5,195 m) of climbing and 21,970 feet (6,700 m) of descents in between. About one-quarter of the time, riders and horses are traveling in the dark. The trail, which is remote and steep, passes through the site of the 1960 Winter Olympics and in places follows old gold and silver mining routes. Temperatures during the course of the ride range from 40°F to 120°F (4.4°C to 48.9°C).

◡ The average time to finish the Tevis is 13 hours, 36 minutes. The fastest time (10:46) was logged in 1981 by Boyd Zontelli riding Rushcreek Hans.

◡ The famous endurance ride was started by Auburn businessman Wendell Robie, who loved riding in the Sierras.

◡ Everyone who finishes with a fit mount receives a silver completion award buckle.

◡ The Tevis Cup is presented to the rider who finishes with a fit horse in the fastest time.

◡ The Haggin Cup goes to whichever of the first ten to complete the ride with the horse being judged to have finished in the best physical condition.

◡ Women edge out men in Tevis wins: women have won 51 awards, men 39. Donna Fitzgerald on Witezarif holds the record for the most wins (6). In 1982 and 1983, Marjorie Pryor won the Tevis on Fritz, a horse who is blind in one eye. In 1991 and 1996, Erin McChesney and her homebred horse, Cougar's Fete, won both the Tevis and Haggin Cups.

◡ The record for completions by a single horse was established in 1998 by Thunders Lightning Bar, a 20-year-old Quarter Horse mare, who finished the race that year for the thirteenth time.

◡ Of horses who have won the Tevis 82 percent are Arabians. Arabian crosses account for 6 percent of wins.

◡ The average age of an equine Tevis winner is nine years old. The youngest horse to win was six. The oldest to win the Tevis was 16 and the Haggin Cup, 14.

HORSEBALL

Horseball, a mounted game invented in France in the late 1970s, has been compared to a cross between rugby and basketball on horseback! Two teams, of four players each, attempt to score a goal by passing the ball through basketball-type rings, which are mounted vertically at either end of a riding arena. The ball is a soccer ball with six leather handles attached.

The riding is fast paced, and before a goal is scored, at least three passes between three different riders must be completed. The ball is sometimes passed with both hands, but if it is dropped, it must be picked up by a player while still mounted and riding.

The sport teaches riders to depend on their seat, legs, and balance instead of relying on their hands to control the horse. Dressage training for both horse and rider is used to develop the necessary communication between them and to teach pace control. Horseball doesn't require elaborate equipment or an expensive course, and almost any forward, well-trained horse can play. The rough and tumble of the sport is attractive to boys, who tend to drop riding during the teen or preteen years. It also teaches horses to be mannerly and to respond to their riders, even in the thick of a herd of other horses.

STEEPLECHASING

Steeplechasing (or National Hunt Racing as it is called in England) originated in Ireland. The Irish referred to early steeplechases as "pounding matches" because they were no-holds-barred gallops across rough ground, until all but the winner—sometimes the last left standing—were "pounded" into the ground.

The term steeplechasing referred to the visible landmarks, often church steeples, that served as winning posts for the early races.

AFGHAN "POLO"

Bushkazi is a traditional Afghan game—a little like polo, only a lot earthier—played by horsemen of the Asian steppes. These nomadic men probably did not learn to ride in an arena, and they like their horsemanship to be dangerous!

The "ball," made from the carcass of a goat or calf—soaked in water, beheaded, eviscerated, and legs removed from the knee down—is called a "boz." The field of play has a pit, surrounded by a circle in the center (the "hallah," or circle of justice). At either end of the field—usually very large to allow plenty of galloping room—is a pole. The object of the game is to steal the boz from the pit, gallop the length of the field on both ends, circling the poles, and then toss the boz back into the pit. As in basketball, players can steal and pass the boz to each other. The boz cannot be tied to the saddle.

The riders ("chopendoz") carry whips, which they can use on their opponents (human and equine), but one of the few rules—not strictly enforced because there are no referees—forbids whipping of people's hands. Horses are allowed, even encouraged, to bite, kick, block, and tackle. If a rider is unhorsed, another rider can steal his horse. Games have been known to stretch from dawn to dusk (or until the boz disintegrates), and deaths on the field of play are not unknown.

THE RULES OF POLO

- A polo team consists of four players, or three if the match is being played on an enclosed ground (this usually only takes place in winter).
- A polo ground measures 160 x 300 yards (146 x 274 m).
- The gap between a set of goal posts is 8 yards (7.3 m).
- A full game consists of eight chukkas, each of which lasts seven minutes.
- Each chukka is followed by an interval of three minutes, with five minutes at halftime.
- A polo pony can play no more than two chukkas in one day.
- There is no height limit for polo ponies.

TENT PEGGING

Tent pegging is a game of equestrian skill that has been practiced since 4 B.C. It may have begun in India as a training tool for cavaliers facing mounted elephants. These riders needed to develop the necessary horseback agility and manual dexterity to drive a sharp peg beneath the sensitive toenail of the elephant and so disable it (the elephant would rear).

In tent pegging, a rider at a gallop uses a sword or lance to stab, grab, and carry away a small ground target—the "tent peg." Variations of tent pegging, all ridden from the gallop, include:

- LEMON STICKING (rider pierces or even slices a lemon hanging from a cord or sitting on a platform)
- QUINTAIN TILTING (rider impales a mannequin swinging from a cord)
- RING JOUSTING (rider passes the point of his weapon through a ring)
- PARTHIAN (mounted archery).

Tent pegging, along with chariot driving, was one of the featured games at the ancient Circus Maximus in Rome. Today, tent pegging is particularly popular in Afghanistan, Pakistan, India, Australia, and Great Britain.

THE HUNT

CN INTERNATIONAL GRAND PRIX WINNERS

YEAR	RIDER/COUNTRY	HORSE
2007	Eric Lamaze CAN	Hickstead
2006	Eugenie Angot FRA	Cigale du Tallis
2005	Beezie Madden USA	Judgement
2004	Jos Lansink BEL	Cumano
2003	Otto Becker DEU	Dobels Cento
2002	Ludger Beerbaum DEU	Goldfever 3
2001	Rodrigo Pessoa BRA	Gandini Lianos
2000	Rodrigo Pessoa BRA	Gandini Lianos
1999	Rene Tebbel DEU	Radiator
1998	Nick Skelton GBR	Virtual Village Hopes Are High
1997	Leslie Burr-Howard USA	S'Blieft
1996	Peter Charles IRL	La Ina
1995	Michael Whitaker GBR	Everest Two-Step
1994	John Whitaker GBR	Everest Grannusch
1993	Nick Skelton GBR	Everest Dollar Girl
1992	John Whitaker GBR	Henderson Gammon
1991	Ian Millar CAN	Big Ben
1990	Otto Becker DEU	Optibeurs Pamina
1989	Michael Whitaker GBR	Next Mon Santa
1988	George Morris USA	Rio
1987	Ian Millar CAN	Big Ben
1986	John Whitaker GBR	Next Milton
1985	Nick Skelton GBR	Everest St. James
1984	Heidi Robbiani CH	Jessica V
1983	Norman Dello Joio USA	I Love You
1982	Malcolm Pyrah GBR	Towerlands Anglezarke
1981	David Broome GBR	Queens Way Philco

RACEHORSES
WHO DISAPPEARED

Top racehorses are worth a great deal of money, and so represent prime targets for thieves, who are often hoping to receive a huge ransom. Most offenders are caught and justly punished, but not all mysteries surrounding the disappearance of racehorses are solved, nor do the stories always end happily.

SHERGAR: Perhaps the most blatant crime involving a racehorse was the theft of Shergar, Europe's 1981 Horse of the Year and winner of the Epsom Derby by 10 lengths—a record margin. In 1983, Shergar was kidnapped from the Aga Khan's Ballymany stud farm in County Kildare, Ireland, by gun-toting bandits in ski masks. They forced Shergar's groom to help them load the stallion into a trailer, then drove away. The criminal investigation was hampered because the thieves had abducted Shergar on the day of the biggest horse sale in Ireland, so the roads were full of horse trailers, obscuring the one that held Shergar. The kidnappers demanded a reported ransom of £5 million, but it was never paid— the syndicate who owned Shergar said that if they paid, all racehorses would be prime targets for abduction. The generally accepted story is that Shergar was abducted by the IRA, who killed the prize racehorse once their ransom plans failed. However, as Shergar's remains have never been found, the insurance company refused to pay out, claiming that he could still be alive.

CORRIDA: The filly who twice won the Prix de l'Arc de Triomphe, France's premier race, disappeared from her field in Normandy following the Allied invasion of Normandy on D-Day during World War II. She was never found.

FANFRELUCHE: Here, at least, is one equine crime story with a happy ending. In June 1977, this Canadian-bred Champion Thoroughbred racehorse, winner of the Eclipse Award for outstanding three-year-old filly, was abducted from Claiborne Farm in Kentucky, while she was in foal to Secretariat. Five months later, the FBI found her on a small farm in Tompkinsville in the same state. The owners claimed they had found her wandering along a quiet rural road near the Tennessee border. When Fanfreluche's foal was born, he was named Sain et Sauf (Safe and Sound). Fanfreluche died in 1999, thankfully of old age.

OLYMPIC GOLD MEDALISTS IN SHOW JUMPING

YEAR	CITY	RIDER	COUNTRY
1900	Paris	Aimé Haageman	Belgium
1912*	Stockholm	Jean Cariou	France
1920	Antwerp	Tommaso Lequio di Assaba	Italy
1924	Paris	Alphonse Gemuseus	Switzerland
1928	Amsterdam	Frantisek Ventura	Czechoslovakia
1932	Los Angeles	Takeichi Nishi	Japan
1936	Berlin	Kurt Hasse	Germany
1948	London	Humberto Mariles Cortes	Mexico
1952	Helsinki	Pierre Jonquères d'Oriola	France
1956	Melbourne**	Hans-Günter Winkler	Germany
1960	Rome	Raymondo d'Inzeo	Italy
1964	Tokyo	Pierre Jonquères d'Oriola	France
1968	Mexico City	William Steinkraus	United States
1972	Munich	Graziano Mancinelli	Italy
1976	Montreal	Alwin Schockemöhle	West Germany
1980	Moscow	Jan Kowalczyk	Poland
1984	Los Angeles	Joe Fargis	United States
1988	Seoul	Pierre Durand, Jr	France
1992	Barcelona	Ludger Beerbaum	Germany
1996	Atlanta	Ulrich Kirchhoff	Germany
2000	Sydney	Jeroen Dubbeldam	Netherlands
2004	Athens	Rodrigo Pessoa	Brazil

* Show jumping was not included in the program in 1904 and 1908.

** Because there was a six-month quarantine for horses entering Australia at the time, the equine section of the Olympics was held very far from the rest of the action—in Stockholm, Sweden.

SOME OLYMPIC EQUESTRIAN TRIVIA

At the 1932 Summer Olympics (held in Los Angeles, CA/Lake Placid, NY), the only Japanese winner of an Olympic equestrian medal was Takeichi Nishi (Baron Nishi), who won the show-jumping gold medal on his horse Uranus.

At the 2000 Sydney Olympics, Virginia's David O'Connor and his Thoroughbred, Custom Made, won the gold medal in Three Day Eventing, ending a 25-year U.S. gold medal dry streak in that challenging equestrian discipline. As an 11-year-old child, O'Connor, his mother, and his brother had embarked on a three-month, cross-country horseback trek that started in Maryland and ended in Oregon. His mother, Sally, is a knowledgeable dressage judge and equine journalist, while brother, Brian, is a popular commentator at horse shows.

CHAPTER 4

Horses in History

In tapestries, paintings, engravings, and sculpture, and in epic poems
such as Chaucer's Canterbury Tales, the prominent role of the
horse in the panorama of human history has been well documented.
Man's association with the horse goes back as far as the Bronze Age,
when the first bold humans decided to leap astride a horse and ride
without saddles. Horses were so crucial to human society that
a simple change in horse tack—the invention of the stirrup—is
often credited with a decisive influence on the rise of European
feudal society.

THE TROJAN HORSE

Despite besieging the city of Troy for ten years, the Greek army was unable to breach its walls—until the hero Odysseus devised a brilliant but somewhat underhanded plan.

The Greeks built an enormous wooden horse and left it in front of the gates of Troy. Then they sailed away, apparently defeated. Overcome with joy, the Trojans dragged the giant horse inside the city as part of their victory celebrations. That night, under cover of darkness, dozens of Greek soldiers who had been hiding inside the wooden horse emerged and opened the city gates. The waiting Greek army, which had only pretended to sail away, poured into Troy, slaughtered its people, and burned the city to the ground.

The story was famously told by the Roman poet Virgin in *The Aeneid,* an epic poem in which he coined the famous phrase:

"Beware of Greeks bearing gifts."

THE HIPPOSANDAL

Nailed horseshoes had been invented by Roman times, but they were rare. Instead, the Romans used hipposandals for heavily laden pack animals that had to move—at a walk (no horse could have gone faster in a hipposandal!)—along the hard Roman roads. Hipposandals—from the Greek word *hippo,* meaning "horse"—were temporary, removable, flat metal plates, fastened with leather thongs threaded though metal rings that were part of the sandal's design. Hipposandals have been found at various ancient Roman sites in Great Britain, including Bishopsgate in London.

XENOPHON

A Spartan officer and master of cavalry, born in Athens *c.*435 B.C., Xenophon wrote two books on horsemanship—*Hippike* and *Hipparchikos*—that are still completely applicable today.

Xenophon's works serve as the original basis for classical equestrianism, and his description of the horse displaying true collection has never been improved upon over the centuries:

. . . when he wants to display himself in front of other horses, especially in front of mares, he lifts his neck up high and flexes his poll haughtily and picks up his legs freely and keeps his tail up. And so when you bring a horse to carry himself in this manner in which he displays himself when he is showing off as much as he can, you prove that he is enjoying his work and is magnificent, proud, and spectacular.

PHARAOH'S STABLES

I n 1999, a German–Egyptian archeological team unearthed one of the oldest identified horse stables, on the edge of the Nile Delta, in Egypt. The stables, thought to be those of Pharoah Ramses II, comprised six buildings and could have housed nearly 500 horses. They contained limestone basins and tethering posts, while sloped floors led to niches for collecting horse urine, possibly for use as fertilizer and to tan leather.

KNIGHTS TEMPLAR

The Knights Templar, or Order of Poor Knights of Christ and of the Temple of Solomon, was founded in Jersualem, in 1120. During the twelfth and thirteenth centuries, this Christian military order fought in the Crusades and also protected pilgrims traveling to the Holy Land. Their emblem depicts two knights on a single horse as a symbol of their poverty.

THE PATRON SAINTS OF HORSES

There are at least nine saints said to be patron saints of the horse (listed below). Apparently horses require a lot of divine intervention, which is no surprise when you consider what the species is put through by humans!

One of the most intriguing is Saint Hippolytus of Rome, born in the second century A.D. (*hippolytus* means "loose horse" in Greek). The historical Hippolytus was something of a bronc, coming into conflict with the pope of the time and declaring himself the true pope. Today, he is known as the first antipope.

Tradition says that Saint Hippolytus was torn apart limb by limb by horses, but this story has probably been confused with that of the death of another Hippolytus, the Athenian King Theseus' son. A painting by Dieric Bouts the Elder shows the martyrdom by horse of Saint Hippolytus in graphic detail. In Hertfordshire, England, there is a church of Saint Ippolitts, which is dedicated to the saint; during the Middle Ages, sick horses were brought there to be cured.

- Anthony of Padua (*c.*1193–1231)
- Colman of Stockerau (died 1012)
- Eligius (*c.*588–660)
- George (died *c.*303)
- Giles (died *c.*710)
- Hippolytus (died *c.*236)
- Leonard of Noblac (6th century)
- Martin of Tours (*c.*316–397)
- Vincent de Paul (1585–1660)

JOUSTING AND TILTING

Just the mention of the word "jousting" conjures up images of knights in armor competing for the favors of fair ladies. However, in fact, mounted combat with lances—or "tilting"—was just one part of a medieval joust, which also included armed and unarmed combat on foot.

In tilting, points were awarded for striking your opponent on the helmet or chest with a lance while cantering or galloping toward them, but maximum points were awarded only if a knight knocked his opponent off his horse. Tilting was a popular spectator sport in the medieval period and beyond. The horses

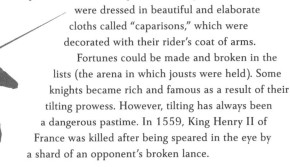

were dressed in beautiful and elaborate cloths called "caparisons," which were decorated with their rider's coat of arms.

Fortunes could be made and broken in the lists (the arena in which jousts were held). Some knights became rich and famous as a result of their tilting prowess. However, tilting has always been a dangerous pastime. In 1559, King Henry II of France was killed after being speared in the eye by a shard of an opponent's broken lance.

THE PROPHET'S THUMBPRINT

This is an indentation often present on the chest or neck of a horse. Legend has it that Mohammed tested his Arabians by letting them go thirsty, then releasing them near a water hole. Just as they moved toward the water he called them back with a trumpet; only five mares returned. In this way, he identified mares of great loyalty, fit to be the foundation of his herd. The five who returned were known as "Al Khamsa" (The Five). To mark these chosen horses, Mohammed pressed his thumb into their necks—hence, the prophet's thumbprint still prized today.

HORSES IN THE MIDDLE AGES

COURSER OR CHARGER: Swifter than the destrier (see below), this type of horse was used for more active, practical warfare.

DESTRIER: The most expensive war horse type, often saved for the sport of jousting, instead of being risked in hard-core practical warfare. Destriers were once thought to be enormous horses, but studies of medieval horse armor suggest that it was made for horses of 15 to 16 hands.

JENNET: Usually a well-bred small Spanish horse. Some of the earliest Jennet pedigrees were ridden by Carthusian monks, who were chosen by the nobility as horse breeders because they could write. The English also used the term "jennet" to refer to a female donkey or to a hinny (see page 33).

PALFREY: A high-bred riding horse, often with a smooth or ambling four-beat gait—faster than a walk, slower than a canter, but smoother than a trot. In Chaucer's *Canterbury Tales*, the monk rides a palfrey, and the Wife of Bath rides an "ambler" horse (with a slow gait, lifting both legs on one side together).

ROUNCEY: An ordinary all-purpose horse. This was the the mount of the reeve in Chaucer's *Canterbury Tales*.

NAPOLEON'S FAVORITE HORSE

Napoleon's favorite mount—a white Arab pony named Marengo—was named after one of his victories in Italy. Marengo was captured at the Battle of Waterloo, taken to England, and put out to stud. After his death, his hooves were made into snuffboxes.

THE INVENTION OF STIRRUPS

⊔ EARLIEST STIRRUPS: By the second century B.C., a simple leather loop for the rider's toe was in use in India, while the Sarmatians of eastern Europe used a single toe loop, solely as a mounting aid. In his late sixth-century military work, *Of Strategems*, Emperor Mauricius Flavius Tiberius specifically mentions stirrups, implying they had been in use for some time. However, Roman equestrian art of the fourth century A.D. shows no use of stirrups. Most historians believe stirrups were invented in China about 300 A.D. and that their use slowly moved westward. Stirrups were used by Sweden's mounted Thegns in combat during the sixth century A.D.

⊔ MILITARY MACHINE: The common adoption of stirrups, when it did occur, was a significant upgrade in the Medieval military arms race. Combined with Medieval saddles with high pommels and cantles, stirrups allowed riders to brace themselves and employ leverage—and the force of the charging horse—to deploy spears and couched lances. A rider in a saddle and with stirrups became a kind of horse–man military machine, a far more fearsome object in battle than a bareback rider, or even a rider with just a saddle.

⊔ MOUNTED WITH STIRRUPS: The brilliant Frankish General Charles Martel (or Charles the Hammer) fought the Battle of Tours in 732 A.D. against a force of mounted, stirrupped horsemen of the Umayyad caliphate. The General's forces had a few horsemen, who had to dismount to fight because they did not have stirrups.

Martel won the battle, due to his brilliant generalship, choice of battlefield, and use of the phalanx battalion formation, but he never forgot the close call. After that, he required his forces to fight mounted and with stirrups. He improved his own use of stirrup technology by analyzing the stirrups taken off the bodies of slain enemies. He also distributed appropriated lands to those supporters who would use their new wealth to maintain mounted fighting forces. Some historians credit the stirrup with the rise of feudalism in Europe.

THE SADDLE THROUGH HISTORY

By 2000 B.C., people were riding, either bareback or with a saddle pad made of cloth or animal hide. Use of the bridle and bit came relatively early in man's association with the horse, but both the saddle, and especially the stirrup (see page 91), were much later introductions.

BRONZE AGE: People used leather for bridles and reins. No evidence of saddles.

IRON AGE: The first documented use of saddles was during the late Iron Age, by Moorish soldiers in North Africa.

ANCIENT GREEKS: Rode bareback. Even Alexander the Great (on his spirited stallion Bucephalus) and his cavalry rode bareback. Xenophon, the first great commentator on horsemanship (see page 87), did not like saddlecloths, claiming that the seat of a man in contact with the hide of the horse gave greater adhesion.

THE SCYTHIANS: A decorative saddle pad of leather, stuffed with deer hair and decorated with animal motifs, was found in a fifth-century tomb in Siberia.

ASIA: The first primitive saddles to use a wooden frame (tree) were in use here about 200 B.C. The tree provided a better distribution of the rider's weight over a horse's back, while lifting the pressure of the saddle off the sensitive vertebrae.

THE SARMATIANS: By the third century A.D., these nomadic horsepeople of eastern Europe were using a leather saddle with a tree and a high cantle (back of the saddle), so they could brace against it when they tossed their spears.

THE ROMANS: A bit slower to catch on, the Romans had no saddles when they invaded Britain, but by the end of the Roman Empire, the cavalry used saddles that had four pommels (essentially a horn at each corner) for greater security.

MEDIEVAL KNIGHTS: They further developed this type of enclosing saddle with high cantle and pommel, which held the rider in place and let him use the saddle to absorb the impact of collisions, lance throwing, or sword thrusting.

THE SIDE SADDLE

The only way that women condemned to wearing long, heavy skirts could ride by themselves was to use a side saddle. Over time, the side saddle has seen many different styles and designs, some more decorative than functional.

EARLY 1300S: When the side saddle was first created, women had to sit facing sideways on a stuffed platform, with a single pommel (or horn) in front. Their feet rested on a planchette (first introduced into England by Anne of Bohemia), but this lack of control meant the horse had to be led at a walking pace.

THE 1500S: Catherine de Medici is credited with inventing a second horn, so that the rider could place her right leg between the two horns. For the first time the rider could face forward, thereby having independent control of her horse and able to ride at faster gaits.

THE 1800S: During the intervening 300 years, the two-horned side saddle was given a side rail, slipper stirrup, and ornate stitching, and in the 1820s, a balance strap was invented. Then, in the 1830s, Frenchman Jules Pellier devised a third pommel (the leaping head), which gave a much more secure seat and allowed women to enjoy hunting for the first time. By the 1850s, this three-pommeled side saddle was very fashionable—an offside handkerchief pocket was even added—but by the 1880s, the offside pommel had disappeared.

THE 1900S: The dipped seat of the nineteenth-century saddle was replaced in the early twentieth century by a level-seated side saddle. Doeskin-lined seats and pommels, made by well-known saddlers, created classic styles from the 1930s to the 1950s in Great Britain, while the Western side saddle was fashionable in the United States. Other countries created their own unique styles, such as the Charra in Mexico.

THE ART OF HORSE WHISPERING

Throughout the long, entwined history of humans and horses, there have always been individuals known to have a "way" with horses. In the 1800s, when the ability to control horses was crucial because of their importance to all kinds of work, a cult of horse "trainers" existed.

🐴 The term "whisperer" may have come about because practitioners, such as Irish horse whisperer Daniel Sullivan, were said to stand facing the horse, close to its head, and it seemed as if they were whispering to it.

> *For what the horse does under compulsion . . . is done without understanding; and there is no beauty in it either, any more than if one should whip and spur a dancer.*
> XENOPHON (C.435–C.354 B.C.), SPARTAN OFFICER

🐴 The Society of the Horseman's Word was a secretive network of horsemen that was at its height in northeast Scotland and eastern England about 1870. Similar to the freemasons, the society practiced initiation rituals, used passwords and undisclosed oaths, and kept its practices and teachings secret, only to be divulged to a chosen few men. Society members made specific claims to possessing magic words and talismans that conferred them special control over horses—and they promoted themselves as horse warlocks of a sort. The secret words were supposedly revealed only to initiates, but phrases or oaths are known to have included the ominous-sounding "Sic iubeo" (Thus I command) and "Both in one," to emphasize mystical unity between man and horse.

🐴 James Herriot (nom de plume of Yorkshire Dales veterinarian Alf Wight, in rural practice from the 1930s to the 1970s) told the story of Cliff, the elderly horseman who helped Herriot calm a fractious draft horse. Cliff faced the horse, grasping the bridle with both hands, and, with his face held close to that of the horse, directed a muttered soliloquy of mingled abuse and praise at the animal that seemed to fascinate and charm him. Herriot (a Scotsman who may have been familiar with the lore of the horse whisperer) noted that Cliff so calmed the horse that Herriot could work as though on an anatomical specimen.

Monty Roberts, Tom and Ray Dorrance, John and Josh Lyons, Pat Parelli, GaWaNi Pony Boy, Leslie Desmond, and others, are such talented trainers that their abilities can seem magical; yet they all have a thorough knowledge of horses, and training systems that they are able to teach clearly.

Robert Redford directed and starred in the movie of Nicholas Evans's highly acclaimed novel *The Horse Whisperer,* which *Cosmopolitan* called "A love story, a gripping adventure, and an emotionally charged tale of redemption and human strength." Filmed mostly in Montana, and costing an estimated $75 million, it starred Robert Redford as Tom Booker—the horse whisperer—and Scarlett Johansson as 14-year-old Grace MacLean, traumatized after an horrific accident that killed her friend Judith and her horse Gulliver, and left her own horse Pilgrim badly injured.

HORSE WHISPERER'S CHARMS

• TALISMAN NO. 1: Kill a toad and hang it on a whitethorn bush to dry. After it has dried, bury the dessicated toad in an anthill for a month until it is a skeleton. At the full moon, take the toad skeleton and cast it into a running stream. The pelvis bone should separate from the skeleton and float upstream; the pelvis bone so obtained becomes the talisman.

• TALISMAN NO. 2: The milt (see page 15) was another occult talisman of horse whisperers. This liverlike piece of tissue, found in the foal's mouth at birth, has never been seen by many horsemen because foals often swallow it, but in olden days, horse whisperers made a point of extracting the milt immediately from the foal's mouth at birth so that it could be dried and saved as a charm.

QUEENS AND HORSE WHISPERERS

Queens are not known to be easily impressed, but they appear to be absolute suckers for wild horse tamers. Both Queen Victoria and Queen Elizabeth II have spent a lot of time in the company of horse "gentlers"—Queen Victoria with John Solomon Rarey, Queen Elizabeth with Monty Roberts.

Both Rarey and Monty Roberts became famous and wealthy thanks to royal patronage and the ensuing publicity, but their reputations were well earned, because they both promoted reasonable, intelligent, and gentle methods of horse training.

Queen Victoria once invited Rarey to a royal wedding, where guests watched him lay a savage horse down on the ground, then lie down under its hooves (Rarey's general taming method). She often invited him to Windsor Castle to demonstrate his skill.

John Solomon Rarey (1827–66) was an Ohio native and author of *The Complete Horse Tamer*. His methods were based on showing the horse that it had nothing to fear from man; he

frequently accomplished this by tying up a leg of the horse so that it was unable to resist, then caressing it gently. This same method was used in *The Horse Whisperer* (see page 95), where Tom Booker lays the traumatized Pilgrim on the ground, then has Grace touch the horse, caress it, and sit on it. Rarey was particularly famed for gentling Cruiser, a racehorse stallion so ferocious that his owners, who wanted to breed him because of his excellent bloodlines, were going to blind him. Until Rarey worked with him, Cruiser had to wear a heavy metal muzzle to stop him attacking stable workers.

Queen Elizabeth has been known to invite Monty to tea so they could have a private chat together, and many times she has arranged for clinics where Roberts has demonstrated his methods to British audiences.

TEDDY ROOSEVELT AND THE ROUGH RIDERS

The Rough Riders was the name given to the first U.S. Volunteer Cavalry regiment, organized by Teddy Roosevelt during the Spanish–American war (1898). Despite the swaggering name, during their famous charge of San Juan Hill in Cuba, the only Rough Rider actually supplied with a horse was Teddy, and he had to dismount during the charge because his horse tired.

Teddy Roosevelt was also an avid polo player, although he was knocked out cold during a match on more than one occasion. During his tenure in the White House, legend has it that he once decided to get some fresh air and embarked on a 98-mile (158-km) horseback ride from the White House to northern Virginia and back during terrible winter weather. On returning to the Oval Office, he settled down refreshed and comfortable for a late dinner.

WILD WEST WOMEN

The wilderness of the Wild West was partially tamed by hard-riding women on their prized (although occasionally stolen, by the ladies themselves) steeds. It was a tough life—many died, some turned to crime. A sensationalist press—and later Hollywood—glamorized their exploits.

ANNIE OAKLEY (1860–1926): Phoebe Mosey, born in Ohio, became the sharpshooting star Annie Oakley in Buffalo Bill Cody's Wild West show—posters advertised the 5-foot (152-cm)-tall girl as "Little Sure Shot." In one of her amazing feats, she'd "split a playing card edge on, then put five or six more holes in it before it touched the ground." Oakley was the first American female superstar, immortalized on stage (1946) and screen (1950) by the hit musical *Annie Get Your Gun* (starring Ethel Merman and Betty Hutton, respectively), as well as in the *Annie Oakley* television series (1954–56), starring Gail Davis.

CALAMITY JANE (1852–1903): Martha Jane Cannary-Burke, born in Missouri, was a frontierswoman, scout (famed for fighting Native Americans), and friend of Wild Bill Hickok. She settled in Deadwood, South Dakota, in the Black Hills, later touring Buffalo Bill's Wild West show. Her life is a staple of popular culture, including fame in *Deadwood Dick* comics; Larry McMurtry's *Buffalo Girls* (1990); HBO's television series *Deadwood*; *The Plainsman* (1936), with Gary Cooper as Hickok and Jean Arthur as Jane; the 1953 musical *Calamity Jane*, starring Doris Day; and as the name of a country-pop female quartet.

CATTLE ANNIE & LITTLE BRITCHES: After Anna McDoulet (b.1879 in Kansas) met Jennie Stevens (b.1879 in Missouri) at a dance in Oklahoma in 1893, they rode the outlaw trails for only two short years—infamous for peddling spirits to Native Americans and also for stealing horses. In 1895, they were sentenced to reform school. It is not certain what happened to them in later life—perhaps they went "straight."

JILLAROOS: Australia's cowgirls (male counterparts are called Jackaroos) traditionally train as stockwomen, before becoming cattle station managers.

THE MEDICINE HAT HORSES

The Medicine Hat horses of Native American lore are almost totally white in body, but have color patches covering the ears and top of the head—the "medicine hat." If they have color on the chest, it is referred to as a "shield."

Horses so marked were highly prized by Comanche warriors; personal symbols were often painted on the white bodies of the horses to strengthen their alleged supernatural power. A circle painted around the eye was known as the "see better" ring. Zigzag stripes painted from the horse's poll (top of the head) down to the hooves were the "go faster" stripes, which symbolized lightning (meaning speed and power). Painted hoof prints kept track of the number of enemy horses the rider–horse team had captured in raids, while "battle scars," for the number of battles the horse had seen, were painted in red.

MOUNTED GENERALS OF WASHINGTON, D.C.

Washington, D.C., is home to at least 30 equestrian statues, mostly generals:

- Simon Bolivar
- Ulysses S. Grant
- Andrew Jackson
- George B. McClellan
- Philip Sheridan
- William Tecumseh Sherman
- George Washington

WASHINGTON AND JEFFERSON

George Washington, first U.S. president and "father" of his country, was a member of the Williamsburg, Virginia, jockey club. Thomas Jefferson called him the best horseman of his era.

Jefferson may have been speaking ruefully—allthough himself a fine horseman, he had a bit of a reputation for riding wipeouts.

◯ In 1781, his horse Caractacus threw him, resulting in a broken arm.
◯ When Jefferson was in his 70s, his horse Eagle was frightened by a deer and Jefferson had another fall, which was serious enough to be noted in the annals of the time.

◯ Toward the end of his life, when he was in his 80s, and again riding Eagle, Jefferson was swept off his horse while fording a stream. He almost drowned, but saved himself when he managed to grab Eagle's bridle.

A HORSEBACK EXPLORER

Isabella Bird (1831–1904) was a clergyman's daughter from the north of England. A spinster until the age of 50, she fell unaccountably "ill" whenever threatened with the specter of domestic life in England, but she always rallied to undertake a variety of fabulous horseback explorations, including trips through Hawaii, Japan, Morocco (when in her 70s), over the Rocky Mountains, and through Tibet.

She wrote several books describing her equestrian adventures, including *On Horseback in Hawaii: A Canter Across the Sandwich Isles* (1873), *A Lady's Ride in the Rockies* (1879), and *Among the Tibetans* (1894), wherein she describes being swept into a raging mountain stream on her horse Gyalo.

NARRAGANSETT PACERS

The now-extinct Narragansett Pacer was the earliest light horse breed developed in the colonies. Prized by George Washington, they were small, mostly sorrel horses with a swift, natural pacing gait that they could maintain for 50 to 60 miles (80 to 97 km) per day. The comfortable gait found great favor during the early American era, when long horseback journeys on poor roads were the norm. Founding sire of the breed was said to be "Snip," the stallion of a herd running wild at Governor Robinson's Point Judith estate on Rhode Island.

The Narragansett Pacer is said to be a progenitor of all North American easy-gaited horses, which include the Standardbred, American Saddlebred, Tennessee Walker, and the Morgan horse. The dams of several influential sons, by stallion Justin Morgan, were Narragansett Pacers. Trade between the West Indies and New England was also common in the 1600s, so the Pacer may have been an early contributor to the Paso Fino—a gaited breed developed in the Caribbean and Latin America that is still popular today.

GYPSY HORSE FAIRS

Appleby Fair is a gypsy horse trading fair held each June in Cumbria in northwest England. Granted a royal charter from King James II in 1685, this world-famous fair has been held in the same place for more than 300 years, and is now the largest of its kind in the world.

Other gypsy horse fairs include Yarm Fair (held in Yorkshire, England, every October) and Cumbria's Brough Fair (chartered in 1330), where Fell ponies are sold. The village of Horsmonden, Kent, in southeastern England, is mentioned in the Domesday Book as a center of horse trading.

THE PRECARIOUS HISTORY OF THE LIPIZZAN HORSE

The fate of the Lipizzan horse, the fabled baroque breed of the Spanish Riding School in Vienna, has often been disrupted by political turmoil.

• 1580: Hapsburg Archduke Karl founded the original stud at Lipizza, near Trieste.
• 1797: As Napoleon's army advanced, the horses were evacuated and ridden to Hungary on a hazardous journey of several weeks. Survivors returned to find the stud farm in ruins.
• 1805: Napoleon again threatened, and the horses were evacuated to Hungary.
• 1809: The Lipica region was given to France as terms of the peace treaty; the horses were again sent to Hungary.
• 1815: Napoleon was defeated at Waterloo; the horses were sent back to Austria, and the stud farm rebuilt.
• 1914–18: Breeding stock relocated to Laxenburg, near Vienna; foals placed at the imperial stud farm in Kladrub; Lipizza obtained some breeding stock.
• 1919 and after: The Republic of Austria became the owner of the remainder of the breeding stock and the stallions of the riding school. After World War I, Italy, Czechoslovakia, Hungary, Romania, and Yugoslavia bred offshoots of the original Hapsburg Lipizzans.
• 1939–45: The German High Command transferred mares and foals in Austria, Italy, and Yugoslavia to Czechoslovakia.
• 1945: When U.S. troops marched into Austria in May, the Spanish Riding School director Col. Alois Podhajsky rode his stallion Neapolitano Africa in a display of the ancient art of classical dressage—lateral work, flying changes, piaffe, and passage (all with a single hand on the reins)—for Gen. Patton, who was also a passionate horseman. Podhajsky was aware that the fate of school and horses was at risk and at the end of his performance, Podhajsky and Neapolitano Africa approached Patton. The great stallion stood perfectly still as Podhajsky made his appeal for protection of riding school and horses, and for finding the mares and foals lost in Czechoslovakia. Patton intervened, the school was saved, and the mares and foals were returned to Austria.
• 1990s: The Balkan War saw the breakup of Yugoslavia, and a band of Lipizzans was moved from Croatia to Serbia, where they nearly starved.
• 2007: Croatia's agriculture minister has at last arranged the horses' return.

THE FEDERATION OF BLACK COWBOYS

Founded in 1994, the Federation of Black Cowboys has its headquarters in Cedar Lane stables, Howard Beach, Queens, New York. Their goal is to expose urban youth to the art of Western horsemanship, as well as the history of African-American horsemanship, including cowboys, such as outlaw Deadwood Dick, Jesse Stahl (great bronc rider and Cowboy Hall of Fame inductee), and Bill Pickett (inventor of the rodeo sport known as bulldogging).

Federation members also pass on the nearly forgotten history of African-American jockeys, who were dominant in the early days of Thoroughbred racing. Aristides, the very first winner of the Kentucky Derby in 1915, was ridden and trained by African-Americans Oliver Lewis (jockey) and Ansel Williamson (trainer). In fact, 15 early Kentucky Derby winners had African-American jockeys, with 5 trained by black trainers. Federation cowboys ride in New York City parades and also hold an annual rodeo.

HORSE IN MOTION

Without a doubt, Eadweard Muybridge (1830–1904) is the only convicted murderer who is better known as a photographer of equine movement. Railroad baron Leland Stanford, founder of Stanford University, and Muybridge's patron, helped him beat the rap for shooting his wife's lover at point-blank range. After all, Muybridge had performed an inestimable service for Stanford, helping him win a bet on one of the burning equestrian conundrums at that time—is there a moment, while a horse is trotting, when all four feet are in the air? Assisted by an engineer of Stanford's, Muybridge developed a groundbreaking technique, using multiple cameras activated by a trigger to capture the entire sequence of the horse's movement. Stanford won his bet.

EQUINE EXPRESSIONS

EXPRESSION	MEANING
Beat a dead horse	Wasting time on a settled question
Changing horses in midstream	Changing leaders in middle of a crisis
Charley horse	Cramp in leg
Dark horse (such as in competition)	Unknown person showing promise
Don't look a gift horse in the mouth	When given a present, it's the thought that counts, not the value of the gift
Eat like a horse	Consume large quantities
Get on a high horse	Being arrogant or overbearing
Hold your horses	Be patient
Horse around	Fool around
Horse of a different color	A different matter
Horse sense	Good advice
If wishes were horses, beggars might ride	If wishing could make things happen, the poorest would be rich
One-horse town	Very small town with few amenities
Putting the cart before the horse	Reversing the order of things
Straight from the horse's mouth	Direct from the highest source
Strong as a horse/work like a horse	Very strong/work hard
To be saddled with	To be responsible for something
Trojan Horse	Deception or hidden danger
Wild horses couldn't drag me away	I'm staying put
You can lead a horse to water, but you can't make him drink	Impossible to make obstinate person do something if he/she doesn't want to

PROVERBIAL HORSES

The air of heaven is that which blows between a horse's ears.
—Arabian Proverb

An ass is but an ass, though laden with gold.
—Romanian Proverb

A hard bit does not make the better horse.
—Danish Proverb

Honey is not sweet for a donkey.
—Ethiopian Proverb

Good people get cheated, just as good horses get ridden.
—Chinese Proverb

The horse is God's gift to man.
—Arabian Proverb

It is not the horse that draws the cart, but the oats.
—Russian Proverb

Judge not the horse by his saddle.
—Chinese Proverb

A hired horse and one's own spurs make short miles.
—Dutch Proverb

Don't change horses while crossing a stream.
—American Proverb

I am a prince and you are a prince; who will lead the donkeys?
—Arabian Proverb

When you go to a donkey's house, don't talk about ears.
—Jamaican Proverb

A donkey always says thank you with a kick.
—Kenyan Proverb

Hay is more acceptable to an ass than gold.
—Latin Proverb

CHAPTER 5

Horses in War and Work

There is an odd split in the manner in which people treat horses.

Racing is known as the "Sport of Kings" and fine horses are as

expensive as the most precious diamonds. Yet we have also used

our horses for the most arduous, slavish work, including pulling

loaded omnibuses through crowded Victorian streets in all weathers.

Some British pit ponies lived most of their lives in the mines, never

seeing the light of day, let alone green grass. War horses were cannon

fodder; one Confederate general in the Civil War lost 39 of his

personal horses in battle.

THE PONY EXPRESS

PONY EXPRESS RIDERS

YOUNG, SKINNY, WIRY FELLOWS

Must be experienced riders who
are prepared to risk death on a
daily basis.

APPLY, **PONY EXPRESS STABLES**

BRONCO CHARLIE: The youngest pony express rider (11 years of age in 1861)
rode 250 miles (400 km) a day on the route from Sacramento, California, to
St. Joe, Missouri, going through Utah, Nevada, Wyoming, Nebraska, and Kansas—
and was paid $100 a day for his daring. In 1931, at the age of 81, he rode from
New York to San Francisco on his horse Pole Star. Like many athletic stars,
however, Bronco Charlie was controversial. He claimed to have ridden two horses
to death in the late 1880s during a six-day horse vs. bicycle race in London.

THE EXPRESS: The 1,966-mile (3,164-km) route was ridden in 75–100-mile
(120–160-km) stretches each day. Riders had to weigh less than 125 pounds
(57 kg), because they carried 20-pound (9-kg) mailbags. The horses—mostly
Mustangs and Morgans with some Thoroughbred blood, which were fed grain
for speed—were changed at 10–15-mile (16–24-km) stages. The fastest ride
was 7 days and 17 hours by a rider trusted with Lincoln's inaugural address.
The Pony Express rode from April 1860 until October 1861, when the telegraph
was completed, rendering the Express obsolete and the company in severe debt.

INDIAN ATTACK: Indian raids were a common occurrence. In September
1860, near Diamond Springs, Nevada, George "Boston" Scovell was attacked,
and both he and his horse What were wounded by arrows. The horse delivered
Scovell to the station but died the next day. Scovell survived.

HORSES IN THE U.S. ARMY

The United States Army has always been involved in the U.S.'s equestrian history. Until 1952, its equestrian team was also the U.S. Olympic equestrian team, and its officers were key in establishing the U.S. Equestrian Team (USET).

The quality of horses in the country has also been heavily influenced by the U.S. Army Remount Service, established by Congress in 1908 to breed high-quality horses for the army. Up until then, military horses had been procured by putting out requests for bids and issuing contracts to private breeders, but the Army was dissatisfied with the uneven quality of the horses that they had bought.

The Remount Service was supervised by the Army Quartermaster Corps. Superior government stallions were offered at stud to private mare owners, with an eye to increasing the overall quality of the horses so there would be a deep breeding pool of fine horses available to the military. Many of these horses found their way into the U.S.'s general equine population.

THE END OF THE
U.S. CAVALRY HORSES

The last living cavalry horse on U.S. government rolls was Chief, who served for 18 years before his retirement, in 1958, at Fort Riley, Kansas, where he was buried with full military honors. The last mounted cavalry charge of the U.S. Army was in January 1942, at Luzon in the Philippines. The elite 26th Cavalry was ordered to occupy Morong, a strategic village on the Luzon coast. Mounted on his chestnut charger, Bryn Awryn, Lt. Edwin Ramsey and his brigade were met by hundreds of Japanese infantry. They charged, and the Japanese fled. Ramsey said later that the charging horsemen, bent low over their horses' necks and firing pistols, must have seemed a bad dream to the Japanese.

Late in 1942, during the siege of Bataan, American and Filipino troops were close to starvation. Gen. Wainwright, one of MacArthur's commanders, ordered the faithful horses of the 26th Cavalry to be slaughtered for food. Like so many of their species through the centuries, these horses sacrificed their lives so that human beings might survive.

PIT PONIES

In Great Britain, Shetland or Welsh Ponies of 10–12 hands worked underground, hauling carts and providing power for windlasses that raised coal to the surface.

Ponies were lowered into mines in elevator-like cages. Often ponies became unmanageable if brought to the surface, so many spent their lives underground.

After the 1842 Coal Mines Regulation Act, it became illegal for women, girls, and boys under ten to work in the mines, but the use of ponies increased.

The 1887 Coal Mines Regulation Act mandated inspections of roof heights (back injuries from low roofs were called "rooving," "topping," or "scrubbing").

A 1911 law stated that ponies had to wear protective head and eye gear.

The twentieth century saw a decline in the use of pit ponies. In 1913, there were 70,000 pit ponies worked in British mines. However, these numbers had reduced to 32,542 by 1938, 6,400 by 1962, and 55 by 1984.

CIVIL WAR HORSES

LITTLE SORREL: A sorrel Morgan, originally named Fancy, which Confederate General Stonewall Jackson bought for his wife.

CINCINNATTI: Ulysses S. Grant's favorite horse, was known as the fastest American Thoroughbred racehorse of the Civil War era.

OLD WHITEY: Horse ridden by Mother Bickerby, a famous Civil War nurse.

TRAVELLER: General Robert E. Lee's beloved gray with black points; the horse is buried near Lee's tomb on the campus of Washington and Lee Univeristy.

THE CRUEL LIFE OF BATTLE HORSES

Heartfelt honors were accorded the equine Civil War veterans, but all wars, and in particular the American Civil War, were cruel experiences for most horses. During the Battle of Gettysburg alone, an estimated 1,500 horses were killed, and letters from soldiers describe the hellish sufferings of the horses. One soldier told of a horse with both forelegs badly cut and blood icicles dripping from the wounds down to the ground—but the horse was driven on.

In general, there was little choice but to be so hard. In a battle, it was a policy to kill horses first, because without them, the enemy battalion would be unable to move its heavy guns and supplies. The average life expectancy for a Civil War horse was about six months. Gen. Nathan Bedford Forrest was said to have had 39 of his personal horses killed in battle.

HORSES AND BULLFIGHTING

In Portugal, mounted bullfighting has been developed as an equestrian art, and horseback bullfighting is known as *toureio equestre*. The traditional mount of a Portuguese bullfighter is a Lusitano stallion, and the object of the bullfight is to demonstrate the training of the horse rather than to kill the bull. The "oneness" of the horse and rider is displayed—the two are described as akin to the mythical centaur (see page 123). The horses need to be highly trained, agile, light, and collected—and perfectly responsive to their riders— in order to dance and dodge about the bull.

SHOWING OFF

The horse and rider perform the movements of classical dressage, but in a highly charged atmosphere of mortal peril. The riders will sometimes tie their reins and maneuver the horse with just seat and legs in order to approach the bull, then place darts in the withers to provoke the bull to be more aggressive, which in turn gives the rider more opportunity to show off the classical dressage training of his horse. The bulls in these displays have had their horns trimmed or capped so that they are not lethal. Bullfighting in the Portuguese style is similar to Western cutting, where the object is to separate a cow from a herd— the responsiveness and agility of the horse and the ability of the horse to react like a dancer to every movement of the bull or cow are the same in both.

A BLOOD SPORT

This, at least, is the idealized art of the bullfight, most commonly practiced in Portugal, and now becoming popular as an equestrian sport in California. However, in the less rarefied manifestations of bullfighting, horses are sometimes gored by the bulls. In Spain, some of the less highly trained horses used in bullfights are wrapped in padded capes *(petos)*, but these provide only a superficial protection against the bull's horns. The horses are also blinkered or blindfolded in an attempt to curb their natural terror. This is bullfighting as blood sport, rather than "art." The use of bulls for bullfighting is highly controversial and anathema to many, whether or not the bulls are killed or their horns are capped or padded.

CIRCUS HORSES

From the earliest days of circus performance, horses have been at the heart of this entertainment industry. Circus horse acts can be roughly divided into three types.

HAUTE ÉCOLE: A variation on dressage, in which a horse executes tricks and maneuvers in response to signals from its rider. The style evolved from cavalry training undertaken by military horses from the seventeenth century onward.

LIBERTY HORSE ACTS: Riderless horses enter a circus ring and perform elaborately choreographed tricks or movement routines, sometimes responding to purely vocal commands. In 1897, the famous Barnum and Bailey circus featured a performance by no fewer than 70 Liberty horses, which is believed to be a record.

VOLTAGE: Here, the rider leaps on and off the horse, or performs acrobatic moves, such as somersaults and pirouettes, while on horseback. One of the earliest types of circus horse acts, voltage remains popular to this day.

THE EQUINE TRAPEZE ARTIST

Circus history also features several famous unique horse acts, including a pony named Blondin who, like his human namesake, was apparently proficient at walking a tightrope! Although Blondin's "high-wire" was actually a narrow plank of wood, the act was extremely popular.

THE ART OF THE FARRIER

◯ HORSESHOE MAKING, AN ANCIENT CRAFT: The Guild of the Worshipful Company of Farriers was founded in London, England, in 1356. Today, certification as a fellow in this guild is a high honor, akin to achieving a PhD in farriery. Certified fellows must complete a thesis and an oral examination, as well as present a selection of handmade shoes of their own forging, before they are certified as a fellow.

Farrier's knife

◯ TODAY'S FARRIER: To succeed, the modern farrier must be a highly skilled professional. Before your farrier earned the right to pull that well-used truck into your stableyard, he or she probably completed classes in anatomy and physiology, particularly because their work affects the horse's lower limbs, hoof structures, and equine movement. Your farrier also learned the theory and practice of corrective shoeing, on top of having practical training that enables

Blacksmith's pincers

him or her to safely and efficiently trim a hoof, forge a shoe, and nail that shoe onto your horse's foot, without laming or "quicking" the horse. Newly trained farriers just entering the market often become an apprentice to a more experienced person. Successful farriers must possess manual and mechanical skill, as well as understanding horse psychology and behavior. The work is dangerous and physically demanding, particularly on the lower back. Women are entering the field in increasing numbers, pointing out that a "way with a horse" is far more useful than mere size and strength. Women Horseshoers of America (WHOA) is an all-female competitive farriery team.

◯ FARRIER TRUCKS: These have largely replaced the "village smithies" of old and are equipped with propane or electric generators, forges, anvils, and the tools of the trade—asps, nippers, clinch cutters, crease nail pullers, pritchels (to punch holes in a shoe for the nails), chisels, various hammers, and tongs.

Hoof or cutting nippers

ANCIENT FARRIERS

Farriers, or "smiths," figure in many ancient legends, particularly in Celtic and Saxon societies, where they were accorded a magical status because they worked with fire. In old legends, the god of blacksmithing is called Welund, Wayland, Volund, or Volundr. Wayland's Smithy—a stone, long-barrow chamber in Oxfordshire, England—was said to be the site of his forge. Legend has it that if a traveler left a silver penny and his horse at the old stone barrow, he would return to find the horse shod and the penny gone.

THE SAD FATE OF WILLIAM SKELHORN

Farriers can probably tell many stories of difficult clients—both human and equine—but in the thirteenth century, William Skelhorn had a particularly trying time. Apparently, in the Battle of Blore Heath (1459), during The Wars of the Roses, Queen Margaret of Anjou and her son Prince Henry watched the defeat of the queen's forces from a nearby church tower. Margaret then ordered smith Skelhorn to reverse her horse's shoes, in order to disguise the route of her escape. As she fled, she ungratefully ordered the smith executed in order to preserve his silence.

FLIBBERTIGIBET

Another legend concerns Wayland's assistant Flibbertigibet. Sent by Wayland on an errand to get horseshoe nails, Flibbertigibet (distracted by looking for bird's eggs) returned late and without the nails. Wayland seized one of the enormous stones of the barrow and flung it at the fool, pinning his heel. Flibbertigibet sat and cried where he was pinned, in what is today still called the "sniveling corner" at Wayland's forge.

GUIDE HORSES FOR THE BLIND

In 1999, an experimental program was initiated to train miniature horses as guide animals for the blind. As guide animals, equines have a few advantages over canines, such as their longevity. Training a guide animal is expensive, and blind owners often experience profound grief when a trusted guide dog dies. A German shepherd or Labrador retriever is elderly at 10 years, but miniature horses live even longer than standard size equines and 25 years is common. Another advantage of horses over canines is that horses are less emotional and distractable than dogs. Horses can also see well in near total darkness and they have a wide range of vision—almost 360 degrees.

PASSING THE TEST

Potential equine guides have to be assessed, which includes evaluation of the independent movement of the ears. Although all horses can move their ears up to 180 degrees, horses who are the most successful in training have "active" ears, which swivel around to follow a human trainer walking around the horse.

"Umveg" testing evaluates the horse's ability to navigate a detour to reach a goal. The horses are placed on one side of an open-ended fence, while a treat is placed opposite the horse on the other side of the fence. Horses who are potential guides will go around the fence to get the treat. Less likely candidates paw at the ground next to the treat, remaining on the opposite side of the fence. Successful guide equines also demonstrate appropriate manners when introduced to other horses, suggesting that those who have few issues with their own species will also adapt more readily to humans.

OUTDOOR LIVING

Equine guide trainers say that despite their small size, "off duty" miniature horse guides are healthier when they live outdoors. Like all equines, they are susceptible to respiratory illness when in enclosed spaces with stagnant, moist air. Even in winter, horse owners are advised to be sure that barns are ventilated to fresh air rather than shut up "snug" as people tend to prefer.

DRAFT HORSES AND OTHER WORKHORSES

A dray or draft horse is a large, muscular type of horse originally bred for heavy work, such as plowing or pulling a cart. Before the invention of the combustion engine and the widespread mechanization of farming, these strong "workhorses" were the powerhouse of industries, such as farming and brewing.

Physically, draft horses are built for pulling—they are tall and muscular, with short backs and notably developed hindquarters, and long hair (known as feathering) on their lower legs. Draft horses have a good temperament, and, despite their imposing size, they are known for their patience and gentleness.

Today, few animals are used as working horses, but draft horse showing is popular at state fairs across the United States. At these events, horses compete individually or in a pair (the "Team" class), a trio with one horse in the lead (the "Unicorn" class), or larger teams of four, six, or eight.

Horses are judged on several critieria, the most important of which include their height (the taller the better), how high they pick up their feet (the higher the better), how big their feet are (the bigger the better), and the neatness of their general appearance.

The wagon rests in winter, the sleigh in summer, the horse never.
YIDDISH PROVERB

CHAPTER 6

Horses in Myth

Myths pay tribute to the grandeur of horses by assigning them some imposing and crucial roles, such as pulling the chariots of the god Ares across the sky at dawn. The occasional capriciousness of horses is also noted in myths that see them as elusive shape-shifters, or call them "hag ridden." And, of course, the ultimate ambition of every committed student of riding—that human and horse become as one—finds expression in the ancient myth of the centaur.

CELTIC HORSE DEITIES

EPONA: A Celtic deity from Gaul (France), Epona's name was derived from the Celtic word for horse. She was believed to be the protector of horses, donkeys, and mules, and she was a goddess of fertility. Her horse was representative of the earth's power and fertility. Her influence was spread throughout the Roman Empire by the Roman cavalry, and in Rome—unusual for a Gaulish god or goddess—it is known that she was honored with her own Roman festival day, on December 18.

> *". . . I noticed a little shrine of the Mare-headed Mother, the Goddess Epona,*
> *standing in a niche of the post that supported the main beam of the stable.*
> THE GOLDEN ASS, LUCIUS APULEIUS (A.D. C.123–C.180),
> TRANSLATED BY ROBERT GRAVES (1895–1985)

RHIANNON: A horse goddess from Wales who married King Pwll, Rhiannon featured in *The Mabinogion,* a collection of Welsh myths. Her son disappeared on the night he was born, and she was wrongly accused of his murder. As a penance, Pwll declared that Rhiannon had to relate the story to all who passed and carry guests on her back, like a horse. She was released when her son reappeared.

MACHA: One of three Irish horse goddesses whose prowess was in combat. The first Macha was married to Nemed, the second was killed at the Battle of Mag Tuired, and, in a third incarnation, she curses the men of Ulster by causing them labor pains, rendering them unable to fight.

EMBARR OF THE FLOWING MANE: Mannanán Mac Lir was the god of the sea in Irish, Scots, and Manx mythology. He owned a horse—Embarr of the Flowing Mane—that could travel over water as easily as on land.

GRINGOLET: In Arthurian legend, Gringolet was the horse of Sir Gawain. Famed for his prowess in battle, Gringolet appears in many romances and poems, such as "Sir Gawain and the Green Knight." His name may be derived from the Welsh *gwyn calet* ("white hardy") or *ceincaled* (handsome hardy).

SHAPE-SHIFTERS

THE IRISH AUGHISKY, or Scottish *each uisge* (literally, "water horse"), is a shape-shifting (metamorphosing) water horse whose home is in seas and sea lochs. It lurks by the shore, and is very beautiful—but woe to those who try to mount it. With a coat that is magically adhesive, the aughisky will rear and gallop into the sea and drown the rider. There is also a version of this shape-shifting water horse in Scandinavia, where it is known as the "brook horse."

THE SCOTTISH KELPIE (or kelpy) is similar to the aughisky but lives in rivers and streams, not the sea. The kelpie's bridle was the key to its shape-shifting powers. If bridled, the kelpie could be tamed, but if the bridle should slip, the rider was doomed. The MacGregor clan was said to have a kelpie's bridle that had been passed down through the generations. The "shoopiltee" and the "nuggle" (or "noggle") are similar shape-shifting horses that come from the Shetland and Orkney Islands off the coast of Scotland.

THE PHOOKA is another shape-shifting horse from Irish legend. It is dark in color, and has yellow eyes and a swirling mane. The phooka is not as lethal as the kelpie, but people who allow themselves to be tempted onto its back still get taken for a very wild ride indeed!

SLEIPNIR

In Norse mythology, Sleipnir was the eight-legged stallion of the Norse god Odin and was a gift from the shape-shifter Loki. His name means "smooth" or "gliding" (and is related to the root of the English word "slippery"). The fastest of all horses, Sleipnir was able to carry Odin into battle, over the sea, through the air, and to and from the land of the dead.

THE MAN-EATING HORSES OF DIOMEDES

Heracles (called Hercules in Roman mythology) was a Greek hero, the product of an affair between his mortal mother Alcmene and Zeus, the king of the gods. This demigod's parentage made him unpopular with Hera, Zeus's wife, and the goddess was so angered that she made him kill his family during a fit of madness. As penance for his murderous outburst, Heracles was compelled to undergo 12 labors for King Eurystheus.

As his eighth labor, Heracles was charged with the task of capturing the horses of Diomedes. These beasts had quite a reputation as savage and uncontrollable animals, and in one version of the story, they ate Heracles' companion, Abderus.

Heracles triumphed in the end, and after defeating Diomedes and feeding him to his own horses, he took the now-tamed animals back to King Eurystheus in readiness for his next labor.

AN ANCIENT CHARM TO TAME A HORSE

Whisper the Creed in his right ear on a Friday,
and again in his left on a Wednesday.
Do this weekly till he is tamed;
for so he will be.

PEGASUS

According to Greek mythology, Pegasus was a winged horse that could fly. Sired by Poseidon, Pegasus sprang from Medusa's neck after Perseus had cut off her head. The horse was later tamed by Bellerophon, using a bridle given to him by Athena, before being flown by him in his successful quest to kill the fire-breathing monster, Chimaera. Pegasus went on to work for Zeus, carrying his thunderbolts.

THE UNICORN

Unicorns are mythical horses with long, single, straight horns growing from their foreheads. When they appear on heraldic coats of arms, their horns are spiral, their tails are lionlike, and they have deerlike feet.

The unicorn also appears in ancient Chinese mythology. The first unicorn was allegedly responsible for shaping the world, with some help from the dragon, phoenix, and tortoise.

THE CENTAUR

In Greek mythology, a centaur is half-man, half-horse—a creature with the head, arms, and torso of a man, but with the body and legs of a horse.

The myth of these creatures could have begun when the people of ancient Greece, who had never previously seen men on horseback, first encountered the horsemen of Thessaly, and believed they had stumbled across an unknown life-form.

HAG KNOTS AND STONES

The knots that form in the horse's mane are said in Celtic myth to be the work of the *cailleach* ("divine hags"). The knots in a long mane, called "hag knots," can form twisted ropes and are said to be used as stirrups by the witches and fairies who steal horses out of fields for "night riding." This was the explanation given if horses were found sweating or agitated in the morning.

Horses were considered vulnerable to supernatural attack, and the term "spooking" (or shying) is still in common use today. As protection from evil forces, grooms would hang "hag stones" (stones with holes in them) over stable doors or around horses' necks.

FOUR CHARIOT HORSES OF ARES

Ares, the Greek god of war, was the son of Zeus and Hera. The four immortal, fire-breathing horses who pulled his chariot across the sky were named Aithon (burning or fiery), Konabos (tumultuous), Phlogeus (flaming), and Phobos (panicky or fearful). These horses were the offspring of Boreas and one of the erinyes (furies), as were many other speedy horses. Ares' eager participation in the Trojan War, in company with other gods, is described in Homer's *Iliad*.

BUCEPHALUS

Bucephalus, or "ox-headed" in ancient Greek, was the horse of Alexander the Great, and is arguably the most famous horse of all time. Said to be descended from the man-eating mares of Diomedes (see page 122), Bucephalus was offered to Alexander's father, King Philip, but none of Philip's experienced horsemasters were able to subdue the wild black stallion.

The 12-year-old Alexander, who had been watching the horse masters fail, leaped upon the horse, wheeled him around, and subdued him. Alexander alone had noticed that the horse was terrified by the sight of his own shadow when a rider was on his back. In order to earn Bucephalus' trust, he had simply turned the horse into the sun, making the shadow invisible.

Alexander's childhood triumph foreshadowed his domination of the ancient world—from Greece to Egypt to Afghanistan—all on the back of Bucephalus. The loyal horse died at the age of 30 in the Battle of Hydaspes, and Alexander founded a city, Bucephala (which is thought to be Jhelum in Pakistan), in his honor.

EL MORZILLO

El Morzillo was a black stallion belonging to the sixteenth-century Spanish explorer Hernán Cortés. In 1525, when Cortés left South America to return to Spain, he had to leave his horse behind. The Mayan Indians, who were unaccustomed to horses, honored Morzillo, renaming him Tziminchac and worshiping him as the Mayan god of thunder and lightning. On his death, they made a statue of him.

THE FOUR IMMORTAL HORSES OF HELIOS

Bronte, Euos, Abraxas, and Aithon were the four immortal horses of Helios, the Greek god of the sun. It is said that every day, the four horses drove Helios across the sky in a chariot, from his palace in the east to Oceanus in the west.

XANTHUS AND BALIUS

Xanthus and Balius (meaning "blond" and "dappled," respectively) were the horses of Achilles. They were sired by the Zephyrus out of the harpy Podarge, who had been disguised as a beautiful mare.

Xanthus and Balius were originally given to Achilles' father, Peleus, by the gods, but served as Achilles' chariot horses during the Trojan War. The horses were later lent to Patroclus, who fed and groomed them. After Patroclus was killed, the two horses stood motionless on the battlefield and wept. Hera had given Xanthus the power of speech, but when Achilles scolded Xanthus for the death of Patroclus, Xanthus prophesied that Achilles would soon be killed. After this prophesy, the erinyes (furies) struck Xanthus dumb.

TILTING AT WINDMILLS

In his legendary romance, Spanish novelist Miguel de Cervantes (1547–1616) takes good-hearted Don Quixote and his faithful nag Rosinante (joined by a rustic peasant Sancho Panza and Dapple, his donkey) on many adventures. As a knight-errant on a quest for doing good in the world, Quixote (dressed in rusty armor and a cardboard helmet) battles with windmills, mistaking them for giants.

FOUR HORSEMEN OF THE APOCALYPSE

In Christianity, the Four Horsemen of the Apocalypse represent man's "last days," and are described in the Bible's *Book of Revelation* as shown below:

HORSE COLOR	HORSE REPRESENTS	RIDER	RIDER REPRESENTATIVE OF
White	Victory in warfare	Carries a bow (but no arrow) and wears a crown	The Anti-Christ
Red	Blood spilled on the battlefield	Carries a sword	War
Black	Desolation and hunger	Carries scales	Injustice for the impoverished, food shortages
Pale	Death by war, hunger, and plagues	Is followed by Hell	Death

BAREBACK RIDING

According to legend, in 1840, a handsome white horse carried the beautiful Lady Godiva—naked—through the streets of Coventry, and covered only by her long hair. Incensed by unfair taxes imposed on his tenants by her husband Leofric, Lady Godiva carried out this act if he promised to rescind them. A tailor saw her from a window, was struck blind, ever since called the "Peeping Tom of Coventry." From 1768, an annual procession has commemorated her ride.

CHAPTER 7

Horse-Keeping Hints

Part of the fun of keeping a horse for modern owners is learning the horse-keeping lore that has been passed down through the centuries. "Seeing to the horse" gave generations of men an excuse to disappear into the barn for an hour or so around supper time. However, in modern times, it is generally women who have gained well-deserved reputations as horse pamperers. This chapter provides a few practical hints, as well as some quaint drawings of horse-keeping paraphernalia of the past!

HOMEMADE BRAN MASH

Wheat bran mashes are like equine chicken soup, but don't give them too often, or to horses under three. The high phosphorous content can cause bone development problems in young horses; excess amounts of phosphorous have also been linked to enteroliths—mineral stones that form in the intestinal tract (often around a small foreign body) that can cause colic in a horse.

However, horses relish an occasional bran mash and this is a good way to get some fluids into your horse during winter (when horses often drink less than they should), after a long trailer ride, or for a convalescing horse (especially if you add electrolytes to the mix). Here's a recipe for a single serving:

- 3-lb (1.4-kg) coffee can wheat bran
- 1 cup (225 ml) dark molasses
- grated apple or carrot
- 3–4 cups (¾–1 liter) hot water

Mix thoroughly to a porridgey consistency. Cool before feeding. You can also add the following to the mixture:

- apple sauce
- whole flax seed (preferably cooked), or even a handful of your horse's regular grain. (Take the same amount out of his daily ration.)
- brown sugar
- raisins
- garlic
- a crumbled oatmeal cookie or two (as a special treat).

FAVORITE SWEET TREATS

Your horse may relish fig bars, peanut butter and chocolate candy bars, breakfast cereal, peppermints, root beer candies, granola bars, corn bread, and coke—some will even drink it from the can— but make sure that you allow such sweet treats only in moderation.

HAY FOR HEALTH

Good-quality hay is the most important part of your horse's diet, essential for his health and happiness. How do you recognize the good stuff?

COLOR: Good hay is a fresh light green color. Hay that is brown may have been damaged by water or heat.

DUST: You can check for dust by pulling apart a flake. If a cloud of dust puffs up, the hay is too dusty. Your horse will inhale the dust as he grazes and it will settle in his lungs, causing him to develop a chronic cough.

FOREIGN OBJECTS: There should be none. Look for weeds, vines, insects, stones, even wire. Especially in southwestern alfalfa hay, check carefully for blister beetles—they contain cantharidin, a deadly poison that will quickly kill a horse. To ensure these beetles are not present, use a reputable supplier, who will have taken measures to ensure that blister beetles are not baled in his hay.

LEAVES AND STEMS: The best hay has a high leaf to stem ratio. If it is full of well-developed seed heads, it was cut too late, and will be lower in protein and less palatable to your horse. Hay is optimum quality when seed heads have just begun to form. Hay that is "stemmy" (that has more stem than leaf) will also be lower in nutrition and less palatable.

PROTEIN: Hay can vary in protein content, from about 8 to 22 percent, but most horses don't require high-protein hay. For a horse used at moderate intensity three or four times a week, 10–12 percent protein is adequate.

SMELL: Hay should have a fresh (not sweet), pleasing smell. Check carefully for hard-to-spot mold—a musty smell is a telltale sign. Look for fungusy white or black patches or tiny black spores. Moldy hay can be poisonous or cause colic, your horse will probably refuse to eat it, and you'll be left with a lot of useless hay.

TEMPERATURE: Break apart a bale and thrust your hand into the middle—it should not be hot. Heat means the hay was wet when baled and it has started to ferment. Damp, fermenting hay can get hot enough to self-ignite. Bales that are very heavy in comparison to others in a load of hay are probably damp and moldy and should be discarded or at least carefully checked before feeding.

TEXTURE: Hay should feel somewhat soft and pliable to your hand, not harsh and coarse. If it feels like a mass of sticks to you, your horse probably will agree.

HOMEMADE FLY SPRAYS

Store-bought fly spray is expensive and can be irritating to equine skin. Here is an inexpensive, safe, and reasonably effective home brew alternative:

- 6 full caps Avon Skin So Soft
- 1 cup (225 ml) white vinegar
- good squirt of Ivory liquid soap

Pour into a washed-out spray bottle saved from your last purchase of store-bought fly spray.
Other popular add-ins include:

- Listerine
- eucalyptus oil
- citronella oil

Fly net

Spray bottle

For the ultimate homemade fly spray, combine the following ingredients. This smells so good you can practically use it as perfume!

- 2 cups (450 ml) apple cider vinegar
- 2 cups (450 ml) cold prepared herbal tea, such as chamomile or sage
- 20 drops eucalyptus oil
- 20 drops citronella oil
- 10 drops lavender oil
- 10 drops tea tree oil
- 10 drops cedar oil
- 20 drops emulsifier, such as polysorbate 20

TAIL RUB RELIEF

A mixture of baby oil and mouthwash rubbed into the dock of the tail with a washcloth can help soothe the itchy spots that your horse has been rubbing.

A GOOD STAIN REMOVER

You can use white vinegar, diluted on a washcloth, to remove grass or manure stains from your horse.

APPLE CIDER VINEGAR

Old-timers advocate feeding apple cider vinegar to horses to aid in fly control. Up to ¼ cup (60 ml) can be added to the horse's feed, or up to a tablespoon to the water.

PROTECTIVE HORSE SUIT

Your horse will be ready for anything in this horse suit, which can be made from nylon, jute, or wool. However, to keep your horse warm and protect it from wind and cold, a horse blanket or rug, made to fit around a horse's body—from chest to rump—is standard. Horse blankets are available in different weights for various weather conditions, and some are waterproof.

A "HORSE" SHAMPOO

If it's been very wet out and you're concerned about ringworm or rainrot, try washing susceptible areas on your horse—such as its neck, withers, and back—with a human antidandruff shampoo. These have antifungal ingredients and are cheaper than horse shampoos.

You can make an invigorating wash for your horse by stirring 2 tablespoons of Calgon water softener, 2 tablespoons baby oil, and 2 tablespoons of a horse liniment, such as Absorbine, into a gallon (4 liters) of water. Apply with a sponge or washcloth to your horse.

MASSAGE TO LOWER BLOOD PRESSURE

Massaging a horse's withers and between its ears is an easy way to actually lower blood pressure and calm the horse. Try massaging the horse in these two areas during grooming sessions to strengthen your bond with the horse, as well as before saddling and bridling to reduce tension.

HOOF SCRUBBER

Use a solution of household bleach or disinfectant and water (1 cup to a gallon/225 ml to 4 liters), plus a nylon vegetable or pot scrubber brush, to clean hooves that have been exposed to very damp pastures or stalls.

COOLING TIPS

FANS: Run a fan for horses in stalls. Standing fans directed at the stall work well, or you can rig up a fan on the stall door—but make absolutely sure that the horse cannot reach the cord!

SPRINKLERS: Set up a sprinkler in the turnout. Horses love sprinklers on a hot day as much as kids do.

WITCH HAZEL: Sponge with witch hazel in cool water as a quick bath.

REFRESHMENTS: Apple juice, fresh watermelon, frozen grapes, bananas, popsicles, and even ice cubes are all cooling and healthy for equines. (Though be careful to limit their sugar intake.)

HOW TO CLEAN A HORSE BLANKET

On a sunny day, drive to your local do-it-yourself carwash supplied with drive-in power-washer bays. Lay that grungy blanket out and blast away with the power washer, then drive it home (you may need a plastic bag or box to contain the blanket), and hang it in the sun to dry. You'll have a clean fresh blanket for less than five bucks, and a waterproof coating on the blanket will not be harmed.

EQUINE FIRST AID KIT

It is a good idea to put together a kit of useful supplies that you can use to treat basic problems. An equine first aid kit should include the following:

 Antibiotic ointments, such as Corona ointment, Furazone, Iccthamol (a drawing salve), Swat (can be used on wounds to repel flys), and triple antibiotic

 Banamine paste (for mild colic-type pain)

 Bandaging materials, such as clean dish towels and washcloths, cloth diapers (if you can find them), disposable baby diapers (they make a good hoof bandage in company with duct tape), gauze sponges, medical-grade sheet cotton, and sanitary napkins (the large thick ones)

 Duct tape (so many uses)

Hoof boots (you can improvise your own with a disposable baby diaper and duct tape)

Hydrogen peroxide

Petroleum jelly

Penylbutazone tablets (for mild pain or discomfort—excellent to have on hand; you can buy them from your veterinarian, but use only on your vet's advice)

Plastic wrap (can be used to "sweat" a leg)

Plastic syringes, large and empty (you can get them from your veterinarian, or thoroughly wash used ones from paste wormers)

Rectal thermometer (tied to a string and a clothespin to clip to the horse's tail—so it doesn't "disappear")

Scissors (curved scissors are useful for removing bandages)

Shoe-pulling tools (such as clinch cutters and shoe pullers)

Stethoscope (to listen for gut sounds)

Vetwrap (ace bandages—nylon stockings can serve as a substitute when you're desperate).

SNAKEBITE

If you live in an area where venomous snakes are common, it's a prudent idea to keep some cut pieces of garden hose on hand in the barn or to take on trail rides where snakes might be encountered.

Horses are usually bitten on the muzzle or face when they investigate the snake, and the resulting swelling can close the nostrils so that the horse smothers—remember that horses cannot breathe through the mouth. Horses rarely die from snakebite, but it can take some time for them to recover.

If your horse is bitten on the face:

- insert the pieces of garden hose into the nostrils and use medical or duct tape to secure them (remember not to tape over the opening)
- get your horse to a veterinarian as soon as possible
- never apply a tourniquet to your horse
- do not incise the bite area.

CRIBBING

Cribbing is a stable vice of horses—a horse grabs a solid object (a fence rail or board in the stable) with his front incisors and pulls at it, simultaneously tensing his neck and swallowing air.

Also called windsucking, cribbing becomes an ingrained bad habit that is hard to break once established. It's uncommon in horses that live in a herd—typically, a cribber is isolated from other horses and often confined in a stall. It can cause a horse to lose condition, as well as be destructive to expensive wood fences—once worked over by a couple of cribbers, a fence can look as if rogue beavers have invaded the pasture. The tendency to crib is also thought to be hereditary in some Thoroughbreds. Unfortunately, horses can also learn cribbing from each other. Cribbers are often constrained and made to wear cribbing straps (leather straps with a pointed protrusion that becomes uncomfortable when the horse tries to crib). The following recipe may help:

- petroleum jelly
- Tabasco sauce
- hot peppers

Heat the petroleum jelly and mix in liberal quantities of Tabasco and hot peppers. Apply the mixture to the cribbed surfaces as a deterrent.

POISONOUS PLANTS

Certain common cultivated and wild plants are toxic. Ensure that your horse does not have access to any of the following:

- Acorns
- Azalea
- Bracken fern
- Buttercup
- Castor bean
- Choke cherry
- Daffodil
- Delphinium
- Dutchman's breeches
- Elderberry (flower and fruit)
- English ivy
- Foxglove
- Jimsonweed (thornapple)
- Larkspur
- Lily of the valley

- Locoweed
- Lupine
- Marijuana
- Milkweed
- Morning glory
- Mountain laurel
- Mustardweed
- Oak buds
- Pine needles and bark
- Red maple leaves
- Rhododendron
- Wild onions

OLD WORMING TREATMENTS

If you think giving paste wormers to horses is a pain in the neck, consider these vermifuge remedies of the nineteenth century:

First, give a bran mash (see page 13). In 24 hours, give one drachm (⅛ fl. oz./3.5 ml) of santonine (worm seed), dissolved in water. Mix in a quart (1.1 liter) of starch and give as a drench. After 30 minutes, give aloes in a solution sufficient to move the bowels promptly.

Or beat together 1 ounce (28 g) aloes, 6 tablespoons of turpentine, and 6 eggs to form an emulsion. Give to the horse after having fed it with two or three bran mashes.

HOW TO STOP A RUNAWAY HORSE

Most methods of stopping a runaway horse are variations on the idea of turning the horse or forcing the horse to circle, but they are tricky and require the unfortunate rider to:

- have not fallen off yet
- retain the ability to think straight and not panic
- and possess a fair amount of strength.

If you've managed to get that far, yet are still being borne away into the stratosphere at a Triple Crown pace, you can try one of the suggestions below instead.

◡ NATURAL BARRIER: If you are in an area with a natural barrier, such as a thick hedge or hillside, see if you can manage to turn the horse toward the barrier, where hopefully self-preservation will kick in and he will stop.

◡ THE PULLEY REIN: Cement one hand on the horse's withers and use the other rein to pull the horse around.

◡ "DOUBLING": Get a short hold on the turning rein, sit deep in the saddle, move the other (nonturning) hand forward, and, with the turning rein, pull the horse's head around toward his tail.

CARING FOR YOUR HORSE

Horse blanket

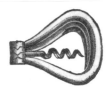

Hoof pick and corkscrew combined

Cotton, duck body feed bag

Tooth rasp

Spring "one hand" horse clippers

Steel curry comb

Mane comb

Pure bristle body brush

Dandy brush

RIDING EQUIPMENT

Metal shoe stirrup

Texas bolted wood stirrup

Friesecke western tree saddle

Cuban steel stirrup

California steel spur

Gentleman's hunting or riding crop

Flexible rubber mouth snaffle bit

COWBOYS' OR RANCHMEN'S BOOTS

The "Montana"

Cowboy's Pride

The Soudan

INDEX

PICTURE CREDITS:
Cover image: ©PoodlesRock/CORBIS
p.45 ©Burstein Collection/CORBIS; p.88 ©Origlia Franco/CORBIS SYGMA; p.97 ©Bettmann/CORBIS; p.99 The Art Archive/Gift of William D Weiss/Buffalo Bill Historical Center, Cody, Wyoming/20.86; p.124 Mary Evans Picture Library.
Other inside pages: Shutterstock®, *The Home-Lovers Encyclopedia* published by Amalgamated Press Ltd; *Weapons & Armor* published by Dover Publications, Inc. (1978); *Montgomery Ward & Co's Catalogue*, published by Dover Publications, Inc. (1895); *Horses – Light Horses*, published by Vinton & Co. Ltd. (1894); *Horse in Stable & Field*, published by George Routledge & Sons Ltd. (1899)

The fly spray formula at the bottom of page 132 is courtesy of *Dressage Today* and Mary Brennan, DVM.